PRAISE FOR *The Hic*

"I greatly enjoyed Joel Rog
sense of adventure and its wo.

—Paul Theroux

"Here is one of the better escape books,
wonderfully stimulating to Huck Finn . . . fantasies."
—*The Anchorage Daily News*

"Prime locations for trips along the West Coast, Canada,
and Mexico are identifed in Rogers' adventure vacation guide. These
spots in the Pacific range from rivers to coasts to islands where scenic
beauty and marine wildlife are abundant.
Rogers' descriptions and photos serve to heighten and
inspire the reader's sense of adventure."
—*ALA Booklist*

"This is my kind of book. I'm going to
enjoy reading it more than just once or twice."
—*Florida Sea Kayaking
Association Newsletter*

"The book describes in word and picture what Henry
David Thoreau called the selvage ends of the landscape,
that part which is neither water nor land, but a network of
waterways created by nature out of coastal inlets, islands,
and estuaries. . . . Rogers is every bit as good a
writer as he is a photographer."
—*Small Press*

"A fine photographer with a nice knack for storytelling."
—*Islands*

"[The *Hidden Coast*] introduces you to remote coastal spaces—
the secluded edge between civilization and the Pacific Ocean."
—*Backpacker*

SECOND EDITION

The Hidden Coast

COASTAL ADVENTURES FROM ALASKA TO MEXICO

JOEL W. ROGERS

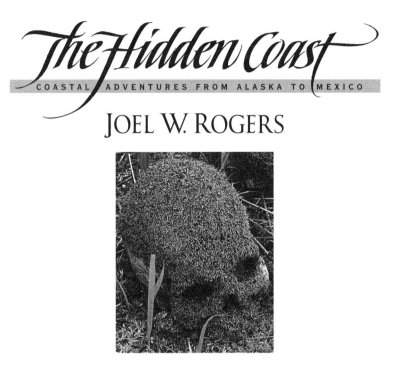

Foreword by Tim Cahill

Afterword by John Dowd

WESTWINDS PRESS™

The first edition of this book was published by Alaska Northwest Books™ in 1991. The second edition was published in 2000 by WestWinds Press™, an imprint of Graphic Arts Center Publishing Company.

Library of Congress Cataloging-in-Publication Data
Rogers, Joel W., 1947–
    The hidden coast : coastal adventures from Alaska to Mexico / text and photography by
    Joel W. Rogers; foreword by Tim Cahill.
       p.   cm.
    Originally published: Anchorage : Alaska Northwest Books, © 1991.
    Includes bibliographical references and index.
    ISBN 1-55868-533-2 (alk. paper)
    1. Sea kayaking—Pacific Coast (North America). 2. Pacific Coast (North America)—
Description and travel. I. Title.
GV776.05.R64 2000
917.904'33—dc21   90-086651
                                                                   CIP

Portions of this text first appeared in the following publications in slightly different form:
"Orca: Johnstone Strait to Blackfish Sound," in Ocean Sports International, March 1988;
"The Translucent Sea: Baja and the Sea of Cortez," in Alaskafest, February 1982, and in Backpacker, January 1989.

Edited by Ellen Harkins Wheat
Book/cover design by Elizabeth Watson
Maps by Gray Mouse Graphics
Illustrations by Lawrence W. Duke
Photo editing by Carrie Seglin and Elizabeth Watson
Cover calligraphy by Glenn Yoshiyama

All photographs by the author.
Front cover: A kayaker's vista of Prince William Sound, Alaska. Inset: A mossy skull at a Haida burial site, Queen Charlotte Islands, B.C. Back cover: Top—Author Joel Rogers. Bottom—Bull Kelp in Johnstone Strait, B.C.

WestWinds Press™
An imprint of Graphic Arts Center Publishing Company
P.O. Box 10306, Portland, OR 97296-0306
503-226-2402; www.gacpc.com

Printed on acid- and chlorine-free paper in Singapore

ACKNOWLEDGMENTS

SEA KAYAKING, for me, is a life sport and a life-support system. Kayaking has provided me the opportunity to meet a unique community of people and to know them as mentors, friends, and fellow paddlers. To these people I dedicate *The Hidden Coast: Coastal Adventures from Alaska to Mexico*.

I want to thank Charley Fiala, Elliot Marks, David Arcese, Glen Sims, and Donn Leber for getting me started, and Richard Strickland and Scott Wellsandt for their companionship on the water. Special appreciation goes to the kayak makers and their boats: Dan Ruuska and his Polaris II, Tom Derrer's Wind Dancer, Doug Simpson and Larry Zecchel for the Feathercraft, and Matt and Cam Broze for the Mariner II.

I am grateful to several persons over the years for both encouraging my writing and photography as well as providing sources for my articles and pictures: Steve Wilson and Karen Hayden of *Entheos*, Bea and John Dowd, founders of *Sea Kayaker* magazine, Carol Ostrom and Ross Anderson of *The Seattle Times*, Ed Reading of *Alaskafest* magazine, Charles Mauzy at AllStock, Larry Evans, Joe Crump, Sally Schwartz, and Sue Smith of *Outside* magazine, and Mike Wyatt of *Backpacker* magazine.

At Alaska Northwest Books™ and WestWinds Press™, my thanks to both Maureen Zimmerman and Marlene Blessing for their ready acceptance of the book project, and to Carrie Seglin for selecting the images and to Betty Watson for designing both editions of the book. Ellen Wheat is the other author of *The Hidden Coast*—she edited the first edition and me as we went along, and she is responsible for the book's return in an expanded new form. My thanks to her.

I'd especially like to thank my friend Sarah Shannon for her paddling, participation, and confidence in me, which helped create *The Hidden Coast*.

CONTENTS

◆

Foreword by *Tim Cahill* 8
Introduction 11

 OIL TO ICE 17
Prince William Sound

 GOING OUTSIDE 29
Chichagof Island

 THE KNIFE'S EDGE 43
The Queen Charlotte Islands

 ORCA 55
Johnstone Strait to Blackfish Sound

 POINT OF CONTACT 67
Nootka Sound

 SOUTH FORK 77
The Skagit River Estuary

 SHI SHI 103
The Olympic Peninsula Seashore

EMBAYMENTS 113
Willapa, Coos, and San Francisco Bays

 PADDLE TO THE SEA 127
The Columbia River

 GUNKHOLING 169
The Oregon and California Coasts

 ANACAPA CROSSING 181
The Santa Barbara Channel Islands

 THE TRANSLUCENT SEA 193
Baja and the Sea of Cortez

 MANGROVE MAÑANA 203
La Manzanilla

Afterword by *John Dowd* 212
Notes 214
Access Guide 219
Glossary 232
Bibliography 234
Index 237

FOREWORD

JOEL ROGERS saved my life.

You sometimes hear this said about the authors of certain influential books, and it is meant figuratively. Fine writers, like Joel Rogers, can inspire and motivate readers. The world, as seen through their eyes, takes on a brighter, harder edge. We aspire to be just a little bit more like the author. We may seek out many of the same experiences related on the page and compare our perceptions to those of the writer. In doing so, our life is altered forever, and most often for the better. This is what people generally mean when they say an author saved his or her life, and *The Hidden Coast,* by all measures, is one of those life-altering books.

But the fact is, Joel Rogers *literally* saved my life one blustery October day just off Vancouver Island, Canada, when I did something incredibly stupid and the kayak I was paddling went over. So there I was, swimming in the frigid waters of Nootka Sound, two miles from any land. Worse, the current was pulling me toward an exposed rock, called a sea stack. Five-foot-high swells exploded against the rock, sending spray ten feet into the air, and I thought: You don't want to go there.

It was a typical Canadian October day on Vancouver Island, which is to say that it was snowing at the higher elevations, while a fine Pacific Northwest drizzle was falling at sea level. As I clung to the kayak and began the process of self-rescue—something I'd practiced often enough but had never done in a genuine emergency—the world did, indeed, take on a brighter, harder edge.

I watched, for instance, as high winds aloft tore holes in the cloud cover so that sunlight fell across the land and sea in purely religious slanting shafts. The mountains were incandescent in the sun, and—more to the point—one of the shafts struck the nearby sea stack like light illuminating

· FOREWORD ·

a saint in a renaissance painting. Swells thundered up against the rock and the wind-scattered spray caught the sun in such a way that I was watching tattered rainbows fall back into the sea.

Joel, who was paddling nearby, called out to me: "Just hang on to your kayak until I get there." This was good advice. The cold water would sap my energy soon enough, and self-rescue is much easier when there is someone there to steady your kayak. So I clung to the kayak and admired the scenery, drifting ever closer to the booming rainbows of the treacherous sea stack.

I was out in the middle of Nootka Sound because someone else had read an advance copy of Joel's book, *The Hidden Coast*. The man in question, the editor of a magazine published in New York, had been entirely captivated. He called me and asked if I could write an article about West Coast sea kayaking. Joel would be my guide and would shoot photos for the story. The editor sent me his copy of *The Hidden Coast*, and I read it closely. This guy Rogers, I thought, is one of those rare photographers who can write. The book was evocative and funny by turns. Joel's capsule descriptions of people he'd met or kayaked with all up and down the West Coast of North America were models of economy and perception. There was also a strong conservation message, but Rogers didn't shake his finger in the reader's face. He didn't preach and didn't whine. Having once been a logger himself, his arguments against cutting old-growth forests in Oregon had a singular and informed force.

Joel's considerable reputation rests on his photography, but his writing—the descriptive passages in particular—were a revelation. Editors and writers generally assume photographers can't write. A better man than I might have called the editor in New York and let him in on this little secret: Joel Rogers is a shining exception to that general rule. The magazine didn't need me: Joel could write as well as photograph the story this editor had in mind.

· FOREWORD ·

But such is the force of the book that I immediately wanted see the places Joel had evoked: the Queen Charlotte Islands, Anacapa Island, Johnstone Strait, Prince William Sound. Like every other soul who's read this seminal book on sea kayaking, I longed to see these areas through Joel's eyes. What better way to do so than to paddle those same waters in company with the master?

Which is how I ended up swimming in the frigid waters of Nootka Sound while Joel steadied my kayak. I managed an assisted rescue, and together we continued paddling to the far shore, where we built a driftwood fire, and I dried out as the snow at the higher elevations glittered in the sun.

If, in reading *The Hidden Coast*, you get the impression that Joel is a man of remarkable calm who is also possessed of a fine sense of humor, you would be correct. It's now about a decade after my little swim in Canada, and Joel has pretty much forgiven me my stupidity (I had been leaning out over the edge of a new kayak, testing its performance capabilities). In fact, the two of us have been intermittent kayaking buddies over the years. We've paddled many of the waters mentioned in *The Hidden Coast*, as well as other nearby bays and inlets and rivers.

The West Coast wilderness—that dramatic and sometimes savage area where shore meets sea—still exists. Move up or down the coast a dozen miles, and there are other delights, not mentioned in the book.

If you, like so many others who have read this book, are inspired to take up sea kayaking, I suggest you refer to the back of the book, and start with those waters Joel rates as appropriate for beginners. Better yet, take a course and refine your skills. Joel Rogers may be with you in spirit, but it is likely he won't literally be there to save your life. Not everyone gets that lucky.

—Tim Cahill, author of *Pass the Butterworms*,
Pecked to Death by Ducks, and *Jaguars Ripped My Flesh*

INTRODUCTION

BEYOND THE TRAILHEADS and tidelines of the North American West Coast lies a remote, seldom-seen, marine landscape I have come to call the hidden coast. This edge between the familiar peopled environments and the immensity of the Pacific is a wilderness of secluded coves, offshore islands, sculpted sea stacks, and nutrient-rich estuaries known to all of us in the abstract, but intimately only to a few. These few are boaters, and especially sea kayakers—a new people of the coast, a returning human presence long absent from these shores, quietly paddling through a water world.

For thousands of years, this thin, rich edge of the continent has been explored by the indigenous coast peoples in seaworthy boats. The Chumash of Southern California paddled twelve- to thirty-foot redwood planked boats called *tomols*. The Native people of coastal Washington, British Columbia, and Southeast Alaska are famous for their finely crafted cedar dugout canoes. But it was the Aleuts of the Aleutian Islands as well as other peoples of the arctic regions who developed the skin boat or kayak.

Rarely will a people be identified for so singularly beautiful and practical a tool. Constructed from driftwood, bone, sinew, and sea mammal hide, the kayak evolved into a light, fleet, supple, sturdy, seagoing craft built to withstand the weather, make the open crossings, and navigate the intricacies of the shoreline. It is this legacy—the Aleut kayak, a vehicle born of necessity—that now returns reborn in the sport of sea kayaking.

The Pacific Northwest can be considered the heart of the renaissance of sea kayaking in North America. Oddly, the Northwest owes its popular love of kayaking in large part to the great Boeing Airplane Company layoffs of 1969–70. There had been a community of sea-touring kayakers in the Seattle area, most notably the Washington Kayak Club founded by Harriet and Wolf Bauer and friends in 1948, and some talented local kayak

ALASKA

Prince William Sound, Alaska

CANADA

Chichagof Island, Alaska

The Queen Charlotte Islands, British Columbia

Johnstone Strait, British Columbia

Nootka Sound, British Columbia

Shi Shi Beach, Washington

Skagit River Estuary, Washington

Willapa Bay, Washington

Columbia River, Washington/Oregon

Coos Bay, Oregon

Heceta Head, Oregon,
Cape Meares, Oregon,
Punta Gorda, California

N

San Francisco Bay, California

UNITED STATES

Channel Islands, California

PACIFIC OCEAN

Baja California, Mexico

MEXICO

La Manzanilla, Mexico

· INTRODUCTION ·

designers and builders such as Ted Houk with his fiberglass Chinook and Skagit kayaks and Linc Hales's Bauer-designed Tyee series. But the sport stayed in infancy until the 1970s. The Boeing pink slips issued to engineers and avid whitewater paddlers Lee Moyer, Peter Kaupat, and Dan Ruuska spawned Pacific Water Sports, Easy Rider Canoe and Kayak Company, and Natural Designs. The first boats were whitewater kayaks, but by 1980 these companies, as well as Eddyline's Tom Derrer, Mariner's Broze brothers Matt and Cam, and Nimbus Ltd.'s Joe Matuska and Steve Schleicher in British Columbia all had production sea kayaks on the market.

Sea kayak tours began in the seventies with Alaska Discovery paddling Glacier Bay in 1972, the National Outdoor Leadership School Folbots cruising the east coast of Baja, and EcoSummer exploring Vancouver Island and the Queen Charlotte Islands.

New Zealander John Dowd settled in Vancouver and in 1980 founded EcoMarine, the all-purpose sea kayak store on Granville Island, and in the same year wrote *Sea Kayaking*, now considered the bible of sea kayak touring manuals. In 1984, Bea and John Dowd published the first issue of *Sea Kayaker* magazine, which quickly became required reading for all who are devotees of the sport.

By the early 1980s, kayaking was growing at an amazing rate; some estimate it doubled each year from 1980 through 1985. Anyone in the region with an affinity for the coasts could not help but have noticed the new sea kayaks lashed to the tops of cars heading off to Vancouver Island or the San Juans or even to Baja. Surveys revealed that these new kayakers conformed to a profile: more than seventy percent had four or more years of college, and they earned a median income of $45,000 per year. They were bird-watchers and environmentalists, ex-hikers and canoeists caught up in the energy of a new love—and sea kayaking can be just that.

In 1980, I had been paddling a canoe and living part of the year out in the Skagit River estuary, when a quick succession of events resulted in my acquiring my first kayak. The key was *The Starship and the Canoe* by Kenneth Brower, the first contemporary "cult" kayaking book, which in part tells of the life of George Dyson and his baidarkas. I was reading a copy while aboard the Alaska ferry when I met a party of sea kayakers returning from Glacier Bay. Their enthusiasm and character were wonderful, and engaged my curiosity. I disembarked in Seattle and a day later I was asked by Charley Fiala, the former director of the National Outdoor Leadership School's Baja branch, if I wanted to build a sea kayak and paddle Baja with him that winter. Without any hesitation, I said yes, and my love of sea kayaking began.

My first time paddling a kayak—the first few strokes away from the steadying hands of friends—was a deceptively simple beginning. The sensation of floating, the motion and glide through the water were intriguingly new. The inherent stability of the sea kayak, something all neophyte kayakers seem to discount, reassured me, releasing more energy and confidence. With my first steering stroke and correction, a course was set. A gentle learning curve began, and discoveries lay ahead that transcended the definition of a sport or the simple traveling from point to point.

Sea kayaking was instantly more than just going places in a little boat; it became a pathway toward understanding myself in the mirror of the wilderness, where my strengths and weaknesses are clear and present. The experience of place—the adventure of journeying to a new shore, the return to a familiar slough, the discovery of an ancient village site—gave substance to my life, creating a sense of belonging, of home ground.

The results of these journeys—the photographs, notes, and memories from the past ten years—have become the basis of *The Hidden Coast*. The kayak trips and expeditions in the book are as much about the character of this coast as they are about sea kayaking. The sport and the experiences seem to have become intertwined—the kayak being so indigenous to the environment it was created for. Perhaps that is the magic I am trying to describe. If there was one clear objective in my photography and writing for this book, it was to tell of the richness and reward of knowing these coasts from the cockpit of a sea kayak.

The Hidden Coast was written for the lovers of coasts, for the ones who wonder where these slender little boats might take them. And it is written especially for those who have already paddled beyond the fringe of civilization. More than anything else, it is an affirmation of why we sea kayak.

OIL
TO ICE

♦

Prince William Sound

Never in the millennium of our tradition
have we thought it possible for the water to die.

—Walter Meganack,
Chief of the Native village of Port Graham

THE BRIGHT ORANGE shapes separate and coalesce, vibrant and foreign against the slate-grey, forest-green coast of Knight Island. As our boat closes the distance, the shapes become individuals—biologists and bureaucrats—fresh from their helicopter, bulky in their fluorescent survival suits. They walk the beach, some taking notes. Others, their feet toeing the cobbles, gather to study a freshly dug pothole rapidly filling with crude oil.

It is a clear, calm afternoon on the third of May 1990, thirteen months after the tanker *Exxon Valdez* rode her hull over Bligh Reef, rupturing eight of her thirteen cargo compartments and releasing 10.8 million gallons of Alaska crude oil into Prince William Sound. Throughout the spring of 1989, the same winds, tides, and currents that naturally flush and feed this secluded part of Alaska drove the oil slick

CHUGACH MOUNTAINS

ALASKA

Coxe Glacier
Barry Glacier
Cascade Glacier
Barry Arm
Harriman
Fiord
Point Doran

College Fiord

Valdez

Port Wells

Hobo Bay

Whittier

Wells Passage

Bligh Reef

Prince William Sound

Bay of Isles

Copper Bay

Knight
Island

Gulf of Alaska

N

PACIFIC OCEAN

with fateful randomness. The oil smothered the life on one beach, missed an adjacent bay, and turned with the ebb to consume another island, another shore in a silent, glistening creep.

In its westward course, the slick traveled thirty-five miles in seven days to foul the east end of Knight Island, invading the Bay of Isles and smothering the beach this assessment team now walks with tons of oil.

The men eye our boat with surprise. Our kayaks stowed atop the wheelhouse, we look like the return of the wilderness tourists. But we, too, are making our own assessments. I go ashore with my cameras to photograph, beginning a document of both the aftermath of the spill and the places it left untouched. Perry and Lois Solmonson, with their good ship *Kayak Express*, are here to check the condition of the beaches, so they will be able to answer the many questions their clients will have in a week when the Solmonsons begin their first full season shuttling kayakers throughout the sound.

The year before, Perry had prepared the *Kayak Express* for kayakers. But he, like many other maritime Alaskans, ended up shuttling Exxon crews instead; he ran the *Express* on contract between the cleanup sites on Knight, Smith, and Naked Islands. We return to the same sites that the previous summer had been choked with boats and barges, floating dorms and landing craft. All that now remains is an occasional oil boom and a pervasive quiet.

Perry at first is surprised how clean the beaches appear, after time, tide, and the roughneck energy of winter have scoured the intertidal. On the surface, the sound looks normal. We hope it has made a rapid recovery. But the pothole at the Bay of Isles destroys our optimism. The oil is not gone, just less visible, harder to get at. It has saturated the basement sands.

In the summer of 1986, I had paddled Prince William Sound on a route just north of here, through Culross Passage to Eshamy Bay and Knight Island Passage. It was July. Salmon crowded the bays and streams; resident ducks, seabirds, eagles, and otters were occupied with young. The habitat was rich and healthy. May 1990, in contrast, screams with silence: there are few birds, even fewer otters. Nothing is moving along the beach, across the sky, upon the surface throughout the Bay of Isles.

The biologists' work complete, the assessment team returns to its helicopter. As I pack my cameras away, an unmistakable high-pitched call brings me around. A mature bald eagle is perched in a spruce tree not more than one hundred yards away. But my relief at seeing something so remarkable, living, is quelled by the oil staining the magnificent bird's head feathers. He stares back, and I retreat, knowing that this bird is dying. For a moment, the enormity of the *Exxon Valdez* disaster becomes personal and focused, as unavoidable as the piercing cry of this one eagle.

When the world learned of the *Exxon* spill, it began to learn about Prince William Sound as well. Continually, the media accounts spoke of this little-known "pristine," "natural" environment tucked up into the northeast corner of the Gulf of Alaska. Larger than Vancouver Island, Prince William Sound is its own geographic entity, isolated from the Alaskan interior, from Anchorage and Fairbanks, by the massive wall of peaks and ice fields known as the Chugach Range. To the south, it is sheltered from the Pacific Ocean by a barrier of slender, glaciated islands—Latouche, Montague, Hinchinbrook, and Hawkins. Within lie 15,000 square miles of calm waters, perfect mountains, and convoluted shorelines still emerging from the recession of the glaciers some 15,000 to 12,000 years ago.

It has only been a thousand years since the first people, the Koniaq—the Alaska Natives from Kodiak Island—kayaked into the sound and settled there. Two hundred years ago, the Russians and Americans began harvesting Prince William Sound's estimated 200,000 sea otters to near extinction. John Muir and E. W. Harriman discovered Harriman Fjord one hundred years later, publicizing to the nation the natural beauty of the sound. During the World War II era, the military punched a rail line through the Chugach Mountains from Anchorage to Whittier, opening the sound to deep-sea shipping. And in 1977, the first of over 16,000 tankers loaded with North Slope crude oil set sail from Valdez.

Today, Prince William Sound is no longer pristine, no longer isolated. It faces proposed timber clearcuts, new recreational development, and dwindling salmon stocks, and it is still threatened by another oil spill. The sound struggles to recover its former richness. Yet, in spite of the collective indignities that the sound has suffered, it is still one of the most beautiful and rewarding kayaking destinations in the world.

I refold the USGS quadrangle to display my intended paddling route and fit the map into a ziplock bag. Next, clothes: I pack fast, weeding out what I won't need, separating what I'll wear paddling from what I'll need ashore. Through the wheelhouse windows, I can see the broad strait called Port Wells that stretches east to the glaciers and mountains of College and Harriman fjords. As the *Express* speeds to my dropoff point, I glance up the strait with anticipation. I tuck thirty rolls of film into a dry bag, enough for six days, and set it aside.

Entering Wells Passage, we cross into the waters missed by the *Exxon Valdez,* leaving behind the three days I had traveled aboard the *Kayak Express* and explored the wild coves and oiled beaches along much of western Prince William's coast. Now the stain of the oil spill, the memory of the damage, and the undetermined legacy can be tucked away, assimilated into the reverie of my own experience kayaking Prince William Sound.

· THE HIDDEN COAST ·

At a small cove northeast of Pigot Point, we slide my kayak off the stern, fully loaded. Lois hands me down a sandwich, and I push off. The *Kayak Express* turns toward Whittier, twelve miles distant. Perry waves, and a moment later they're gone.

My boat for this trip is an aqua Wind Dancer, and it's loaded to the gills. I set my spray skirt tight and leave the rudder up. Using my body and paddle to steer, I follow the curve of the shoreline, warming up, taking my time to get up to speed. There is no wind and a negligible current. The sun above is slowly being overrun by a textbook 1,004-millibar low-pressure system. In this part of the country that means rain for the rest of the trip. This is no foreboding; it's more a fact of life when kayaking Prince William Sound. Perry had talked about the rain as a rite of passage: "You need three tarps: one for the kitchen, one close over your tent, and another inside as an extra floor. When it really gets bad, tarp your clothesline. And make sure you take an umbrella to stay dry when you leave the tent at night."

My umbrella lies ready beside my seat. Nearby Whittier, with an average of 189 inches of precipitation per year (including twenty-one feet of snow), garners respect from a Seattle native. But this low will take its time.

I enter four-mile-wide, ten-mile-long Port Wells and see the far distant entrances to College and Harriman fjords dwarfed by the Chugach massif that rises up out of the sound in the excessive scale of Alaska. In 1902, John Muir wrote about the Chugach Range: "Peak over peak dipping deep in the sky, a thousand of them, icy and shining, rising higher, higher beyond and yet beyond one another, burning bright in the afternoon light."

It is as Muir wrote, near countless peaks, nameless beautiful horns rising to shoulder the great summits—Mount Valhalla, 12,135 feet, Mount Goode, 10,610 feet, and Marcus Baker, 13,176 feet—spawning glaciers in all directions, some winding and falling with frozen inertia into the jade waters of my intended goal, Harriman Fjord. As I paddle toward them, I watch the leading edge of the front wedging over their summits. It blocks the sun until the only color remaining throughout Port Wells is the ethereal turquoise of the distant glacier ice.

Hobo Bay is my first camp. One of a series of bays along the west side of Port Wells, its still water stretches back like a purse into a rounded, steep-sided alpine valley. At its head, a remnant of the glacier that long ago created this soft-edged landscape straddles the ridge. The glacier's onetime terminal moraine sprawls, stranded by the receding ice and isolated by the advancing sea—an arc of earth created by the then bulldozer-like advance of the glacier. Shaped like a spit, the moraine nearly closes off the bay, creating an easy-landing, two-sided, shale beach camp at its point.

I site my tent along the beach margin where the forest begins. The kitchen goes out on the spit's end, where a forested would-be islet provides some protection from the threatening weather. While I hurry to get the stove going, I wonder about the approaching front, the possibility of high wind, the height of the tide, and bears. I make a mental note to tie up the kayak, even though it's resting in the beach grasses well above my tent—I've seen kayaks and tents blow away. The assorted potential problems and logical solutions dwindle in my mind as dinner heats. I find a perfect seat beneath the boughs of a western hemlock and anticipate food, happy in my solitude.

Rain sounds, crows in the trees, periodic cries of eagles, and along the shore, the cackling of harlequin ducks pairing up. It's probably past sunrise, somewhere between 5:00 and 6:00 A.M. There are low clouds, no wind, and it's cold. Bergy bits, the term for small icebergs, drift seaward in the distance. The rain, a steady drizzle, is amplified against the tent fly. I turn from the flap and check the corners of my old dome tent for seepage: dry enough. My mind weighs the options: I'm roughly eight miles inside Port Wells and ten miles from the first of the great tidewater glaciers. I can break camp now and paddle well into the fjords, wait out the rain over breakfast, or burrow back into my sleeping bag.

Grape Nuts or granola? I walk into the relative dryness of the forest after my cached food bag, flushing crows and shaking the rain-drops off the snowberry bushes. Amidst the noise of cloth against branch I think I hear a whale sounding—an orca or a humpback. Quickly I backtrack to the beach and wait, scanning about a mile out. Nothing. Grape Nuts it is, beneath the trees.

As I crunch my way through breakfast, I am witness to the morning patterns of the local waterfowl. Grebes I have to identify in the bird book (red-necked); they fish in ten to fifteen feet of water forty feet offshore. The harlequins, five of them, want to feed along the edge of my fine gravel beach, but hang back, arguing about the threat of my presence. They are safe from me, safe from the oil: Port Wells was spared. It is Prince William Sound just as it should be.

My somewhat abstract gaze falls on something that does not register at first. I am conscious of the movement of two, now three, black shapes rising out of the water near shore. They are dorsal fins—orcas! A whoosh of air, plumes of mist, and the dorsal fins slide beneath the surface. Two females and a young one travel through the space where the grebes have been, roiling the cold waters in their passing with an implicit power that electrifies my simple morning. The pod surfaces again in the same order of appearance: two then one, along the shore edge. I hear their breaths once more, and then my front yard is returned to the smaller if no less important activities of harlequins and grebes.

I return to my coffee, my apropos copy of Melville's *Moby Dick*, and my satisfaction with Hobo Bay. As morning stretches into afternoon,

Ishmael signs on, the tide comes and goes, and the rain softens whatever resolve I have to move on.

The following morning is the beginning of a travel day. Amidst the activity of packing the boat, it's just luck that I am momentarily still when four miles off, clear across Port Wells, comes the faint sound of whales—orcas breathing, two then one. Listening again to make sure, I am intensely pleased to recognize the small pod of the morning before, now traveling along the opposite shore, heading west. I wonder where they've been, if they've traveled and hunted the entire shoreline of both fjords. Just my recognizing them and sensing their possible behavior creates within me a remarkable feeling of kinship. I find myself thinking of them as survivors, glad they had the good fortune or presence of mind to avoid the oil spill.

I paddle into winter. Snow covers all the peaks and hills within view. Snow, in fact, covers everything down to the tideline. Well down Barry Arm, the entrance to Harriman Fjord, the waters surrounding my kayak are increasingly littered with ice: bergy bits (as big as a small house), growlers (larger than six feet across and no more than three feet above water), and brash ice (fragments no bigger than a refrigerator) crowd my path. The rain lightens and I push back my hood, opening up my peripheral vision. I drop the rudder and begin navigating cautiously through the jewel-like clutter, taking care not to chip the boat's Gel-coat.

May 5 is an early start for tourist season at Prince William Sound, but then the time to visit depends upon what you want to experience. Early May means no wildflowers, no bugs, no people, no suntan—just orcas, migrant waterfowl, glaciers, and rain. Snug beneath my hood, hands warm within kayaker's pogies, I am content with my decision to come early, to see the fjords in the final moments of winter.

At Point Doran, Harriman Fjord opens, revealing glaciers winding down from the clouds. I paddle through the thick of a great stream of ice flowing from the calving glaciers of Barry Arm, picking my way to the eastern shore like an ice breaker searching for leads. Three glaciers calve into the arm: Cascade, Barry, and Coxe. Together they form an almost unbroken ice face 150 feet high and one mile across. I drift to a stop at the crack of a serac the equivalent of a twelve-story building breaking off from the ice face. It tumbles like a fainting soldier into the bay, creating a ground swell that rears up in a ponderous wave. The wave makes its way toward me, its energy blunted by all the floating ice. I stay still, away from any of the larger, potentially unstable bergy bits as the wave passes beneath my kayak and rebounds off the shore.

Minute by minute, the sudden report and rumbling thunder of ice falling into the sea reverberates off the mountain walls that enclose Barry Arm. It is an intimidating world, cold and seemingly inhospitable until I begin to pass a remarkable assortment of residents comfortable within this ice amphitheater. The grey lumps loafing on bergy bits are harbor seals; the brown ones are sea otters. Overhead, black-legged kittiwakes wheel and call, while serious territorial discussions take place between black oystercatchers along the tideline.

Matching the natural features of the landscape with the quadrangle, I find a campsite. To the right of Coxe Glacier is a small point of land, just clear of the glacier's steeply sloping face. I beach beside the tracks of a foraging river otter, and pull the boat high.

My time at Barry Arm is spent sitting on a rock grandstand just watching the glaciers. At times I catch a seal watching me, and as I turn it slips beneath the surface. From my perch beneath my umbrella, I take notes and pictures, and I watch the calving ice and curious seals. I have become a resident more than an intruder.

Deep in this pocket of wilderness, I seem to be accepted. My kayak and I move as the Koniaq once did. The otters eye me from ice floes, sliding into the sea as their natural caution overcomes their intense curiosity; they seek protection but without any sign of alarm. The otters' nonchalance is curious: is it because few people come here, at this time of year? Possibly I'm not recognized as a man but a floating, long and pointy living thing with thin wings? Occasionally, I have to speak to let a dozing otter know I'm near so I won't startle it.

Days later I pack the Wind Dancer a last time for the return to Whittier. I have over twenty miles to paddle with the outgoing tide. I sort through the cockpit day bag and hesitate over the sunglasses. Maybe today they'll get some use.

The glaciers were busy overnight: the bay is full of ice, there is no open water. I clunk my way slowly through the slurry. For miles, I rudder and lean, reach out to fend off the bigger chunks, paddle briefly and fend again, the otters watching me go. Just short of Point Doran, I break clear and paddle as fast as I can.

I keep the pace until I sweat, covering a mile in a few minutes before settling into a daylong rhythm. I am paddling back into spring, passing rafts of ducks—oldsquaw, shovelers, and scoters. A flock of extra-large shorebirds sends me diving again for the bird book. Whimbrel.

Along the forest margin, varied thrushes, orange against the green, remind me of the biologists and the spill. I'm left wondering if we will ever know the total devastation of the *Exxon Valdez* incident, measured not just in wildlife losses and the degradation of the sound but in our own failure to save this great resource. And now, in the aftermath, we witness the degeneration of our conviction as the horror of this disaster dissipates from headlines and memories.

The legacy of the Prince William Sound oil spill is a residue of legal entanglements and political compromise. Meanwhile, the moment of this tragedy is passing and with it the momentum for industry, the states, the federal government, and the people to forge a collective attitude and an effective technology to prevent the further destruction of our environment.

As I pass Point Doran, the rain stops completely. By Hobo Bay, I paddle into the sunshine with no regrets for my time spent in the introspective tenor of the rain. But try as I may I can't shake the simple question: When will the glistening oil come again?

GOING OUTSIDE

◆

Chichagof Island

NOWHERE ELSE WILL you find more idiosyncratic machines. Dotted throughout the northern landscape—tinkered, tweaked, and forever welded into some form of running order—machines in Alaska tend to have their own personae, their own oil-dripping character. Bought used, jury-rigged, and worked to exhaustion, they rest wherever they lose their usefulness, only to be reborn again for some purpose their original designers never dreamed of. Until one day they stop for good, oxidizing in a ring of fireweed, monuments to the only land that could master them.

Like the people of Alaska, their machines are anachronisms. They are too hardy, too individualistic to make it in the Lower 48. Huge D-9 Cats bulldoze about Fairbanks like latter-day musk-oxen. Along the Beaufort seacoast, the startling forms of arctic drill rigs, coated in hoarfrost, rise up from the tundra like modern totems.

But of all the truly wondrous machines in the North, it is the bush planes that universally capture Alaskans' hearts. Their plodding, droning progress across the wilderness sky is the quintessential sound of

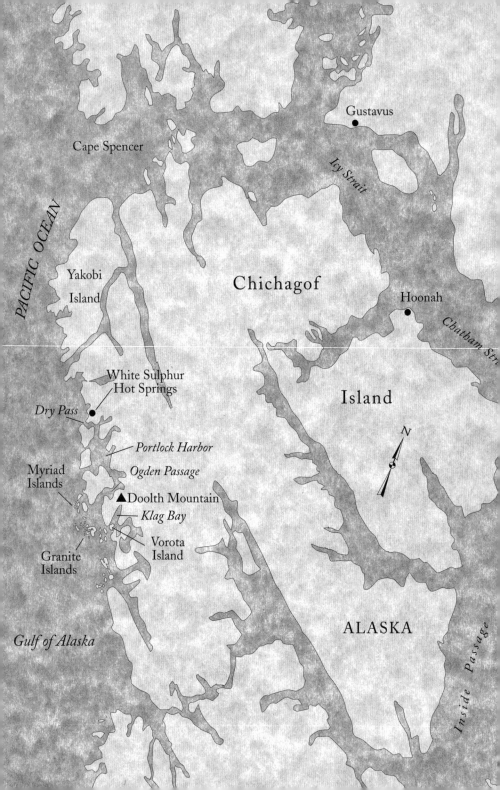

Gustavus

Cape Spencer

Icy Strait

PACIFIC OCEAN

Yakobi
Island

Chichagof

Hoonah

Island

Chatham Str

White Sulphur
Hot Springs

Dry Pass

Portlock Harbor

Ogden Passage

N

Myriad
Islands

▲Doolth Mountain

Klag Bay

Vorota
Island

Granite
Islands

ALASKA

Gulf of Alaska

Inside Passage

· GOING OUTSIDE ·

Alaskan energy. And of all the planes working the bush, it is the De Havillands that hold a special niche.

The amphibious Otter stands ticking with heat on the weathered concrete runway of the Gustavus Airport. While its 600-horsepower Pratt & Whitney engine cools, the pilot skids the last of the Juneau load—backpacks, hard goods, and frozen food—out the portside cabin door and into the arms of the townspeople.

The De Havilland Otter, a big, high-winged floatplane, is the last of the radial engine bush planes, a Canadian design of the 1940s, built in the fifties, and still flying today. With its boxy fuselage, shiny propeller, bulbous engine cowling, visible rivets, and portholes for windows, the Otter would be a museum piece in the Lower 48. But her rugged airframe, a stall speed of fifty miles an hour, and a carrying capacity of roughly one-third her weight are precisely the characteristics needed in an airplane for the Alaskan bush.

It takes an Otter to carry several paddlers and their breakdown kayaks, provisions, and camping gear in one load to a remote water landing on the weather-beaten Alaska coast. We fit in the plane without much ado. The pilot, flying his first summer in Alaska territory, buckles up, and the massive radial engine shatters the conversations in the cabin. I quickly tear the preface page of my trip book into strips, sacrificing it for earplugs, as the plane thunders its way into a south wind and lifts into the air.

The Otter hangs just below a flat, grey ceiling at one thousand feet on a westward bearing. We passengers, strangers for now, isolated from each other by the din, press our noses to the portholes, lost in reading the shoreline. Our introductions at the airport had been hurried. But there will be time to get acquainted, for we are soon to be sharing sea kayaks and paddling perhaps the most adventurous sea kayaking tour on the market, the ocean coast of Chichagof Island.

· THE HIDDEN COAST ·

The pilot alters course to fly through North Inian Pass, taking Cape Spencer to starboard, Yakobi and Chichagof Islands to port. To those familiar with these parts, we are "going Outside," leaving the famous route of the Alaskan gold prospectors—the protected waterway known as the Inside Passage—for the notorious waters of the Gulf of Alaska and the open Pacific.

The plane enters the cloud cover; we strain for last looks, and gaze across the cabin as rain streaks the windows. There are five of us—a physical therapist on contract in Anchorage, a New York photographer, a man who runs a gas station in Texas, our Gustavus-based guide, and I. We all appear to have the same thought: "Oh Lord, not nine days of rain!"

We are bound for one of the largest islands of the Southeast Alaska archipelago. Chichagof, named in 1805 by Russian explorers, covers twenty-five hundred square miles of wilderness big enough to claim its own mountain range. This island is a part of Alaska frequented only by salmon fishermen, winter deer hunters out from Juneau one hundred miles to the east, and the odd prospector. Too rugged, too wet, too remote for people to stick, it has an unwritten history of a few Tlingit villages, eighteenth-century Russian sea otter hunters, beach loggers, and miners, all long gone.

I can tell by the compass we've turned south. The pilot, unbeknownst to us, is searching for a way down through the clouds. It is an uneasy moment, flying blind. The cabin dims as we pierce the cloud centers. The rain increases suddenly, and just as suddenly drops away. A darker patch beneath us proves to be a gap in our cloud floor, revealing a shadowed sea, breaking surf on battered rock, a treed shore. The Otter banks steeply into a descending spiral. We passengers unused to such maneuvers white-knuckle it as we drop through the hole and into the clear.

We turn inland, the Otter descending, while the pilot scans a series of inlets that cut into the island's mountainous spine. He reads the chart and confers with our guide, and then banks the Otter once again and turns into the wind. We land with the elegant smoothness of a floatplane on flat water.

The huge propeller rotates to a stop and the Otter glides to a fine gravel beach, littered with expired salmon and enveloped in a ringing quiet. One by one, we hop from the floats to dry ground and take in the panorama. Toward the sea lies a low agglomeration of irregular islands softened by a full forest covering. Across the still water, salmon randomly leap at the low clouds and fall back with a substantial plop. At our backs, the spawning stream they seek falls through the trees, then meanders briefly through a high grass marsh to meet saltwater just down the beach.

The pilot and guide are already unpacking the plane. We form a chain and quickly unload our food, gear, supplies, and our precious kayaks. In the long, blue bags are the Nautiraids—French double kayaks made with a laminated wood framing and a rubberized fabric skin. I unpack my single Feathercraft enclosed in its own backpack that looks more like a compact red futon. Within lurks the answer to a question breakdown kayak owners on a remote beach commonly ask themselves as the floatplane turns into the wind and effortlessly flies away: "Are all the parts here?"

The Feathercraft has thirty parts. Its frame is an ingenious linkage of color-coded aircraft aluminum tubing that would look and behave like a deflated blimp if one part were missing. I lay them out: bow keel, port and starboard chine and deck ribs, seat frame, and rudder. Piece by piece I fit tube to tube, color to color. Then I insert the bow frame into the very red fabric skin, followed by the stern frame. I lever the extension tubes to tightness and voilà—a sixteen-and-a-half-foot sea kayak, all parts fitted in fifteen minutes, ready for sea. I rest easy, the salmon jump, the rain stops. We load the group gear and our personal belongings, and gently carry the boats to tidewater.

Breakdown kayaks are remarkable craft—certainly the closest contemporary adaptation of the ancient Eskimo and Aleut sea kayaks. Like their predecessors, they bend and work through the waves. Though they usually carry less and are not quite as fast as their rigid fiberglass cousins, their versatility is unquestioned. They make this trip possible.

We paddle for two hours into the late afternoon, covering five miles of forested passes and still water in open, lakelike crossings before holing up on a small island, well back from the ocean. Nate Borson, our guide from Spirit Walker Expeditions, helps us unload the kayaks before we all hoist them above the tideline. A campsite is picked on one grassy end of the island, and our bear-attracting kitchen goes on the other.

As an unseen August sun lowers in the west, we settle in for an all-you-can-eat dinner of smoked salmon, a salad of fresh Gustavus vegetables, and home-baked bread. Between bites, our eyes survey our new world. It's definitely not Texas City, Texas, as Dan Reader ponders how he's going to get his new wool socks dry. To Alan Fortune, who was living and working in Manhattan forty-eight hours ago, it is a photographer's dream come true. And Tamara Beaulieu, just recently moved to Anchorage from Michigan, looks upon this seascape as her new backyard.

I am curious why these people signed on for a kayak trip to the wild and woolly ocean coast of Alaska when they have little or no experience in sea kayaks. Over some Red Zinger tea, I find the common thread is a strong desire to experience wilderness Alaska, intertwined with a love of water, ocean coasts, and a curiosity about sea kayaks. To

Tamara, it's more than curiosity. A long-distance cyclist, she chose this trip not only to see a unique part of Alaska but to learn another way to move naturally through the world.

Nate loves that response. It is his job to teach the beginners paddling, steering, safety, and rescue techniques, as well as to shape us all into a responsible team that cares for the environment, the equipment, and each other throughout the trip. I realize that our combined skills limit us to good-weather traveling and that we might get stormed in somewhere. If that happens, we'll just have to wait for the weather to clear and the Otter to come to our rescue. We talk into darkness this first night, listening to the periodic plop of the salmon, adjusting to being on our own, in good company, well away from anything familiar.

Morning brings a promise of improving weather. As I carry my belongings to my waiting kayak, I take in our setting with a new appreciation. The clouds have lifted, revealing a range of 2,000-foot peaks. One, Doolth Mountain, a curious name from the Tlingit meaning "everything good and plentiful," is shaped like a child's drawing. Standing alone, it rises up from the dark waters of the bay like an inverted sno-cone, cloaked in distinct zones of moss-green forests, grass-bright meadows, and a naked rock summit. A fault, like an ancient scar, creases its southern flank. I can see the tailings of old gold mines following the cleft up over the ridge, mute evidence of the played-out claims of the Alaska gold-mining days.

The low tide reveals our own golden tailing of rock-clinging fucus, that air-filled translucent yellow seaweed that pops when you step on it. Gingerly, we set the kayaks at the water's edge and load amidst the sounds of expiring fucus bladders. The cold sea water presses against my boots, as I gauge just how far from shore I can stand to load my kayak without getting wet. Everyone is busy, carefully packing dry bags into the bows and sterns of the double kayaks. Nate judiciously hands out the divided group gear to each of us. I take the stove, some fuel, and the lunch bag, and pack the food within easy reach.

We are anxious to get paddling, to get to sea. Nate lifts the bow of Dan and Tamara's double off the beach. I drift offshore and watch Nate as he oversees the new kayakers getting squared away—spray skirts fitted to coamings, rudders down, paddles right side up. I find myself wondering whether his is an enviable job.

Over the past decade, about fifty sea kayaking guide services have sprung up throughout the world. Founded by sea kayakers searching for a way to make a living doing what they love, today most of the principals paddle a computer while their hired guides work season-long, seventy-hour weeks, learning to deal with short-fused clients and lost kayaks and not making much more than $3,000 a summer. The true rewards are time spent kayaking, being with kindred spirits, the potential for romance one outfit calls "the retirement plan," and living life in the wilderness. As Nate settles into the rear seat of his Nautiraid, I am again struck by how similar he is to the many guides I've come to know. They are, both men and women, easygoing personalities, with rugged good looks, simple lifestyles, and a strong environmental consciousness. Money is not everything.

Vorota Island: *Vorota* means "the gate" in Russian. It is a stopper island, nearly blocking the mouth of Klag Bay and the placid waters of our put-in. We paddle through the narrow channel like kids going outdoors to play, our world changing with every forward stroke. Before us lie a hundred islands festooned along the outer edge of Chichagof—geologically sharp-edged islands, islets, and reefs showing white as the wind-generated swells break against their granite margins.

Instantly, we are taking wind and chop from due north. I lean forward to zip up my sprayskirt and pull my McCall, Idaho, baseball cap on tighter. Instinctively I'm gripping my paddle shaft too tightly. I tell myself to ease up as I rudder right, bringing my bow back up on course. We're going to get wet. I look back and see Dan and Tamara fighting their first wind. Tamara, in the bow, takes a shot of spray, laughs, paddles, and laughs again. Dan is busy learning to hold the kayak on course; he lets the boat fall off broadside to the wind, forcing them to work harder to regain their course. In time, he begins to anticipate the waves and winds, as Nate shepherds us along the windward edge of the first islands.

This is not the open ocean; the thick sweep of islands and islets off our port bows blocks the sea swell. Instead we are crossing the southern entrance to Ogden Passage, a three-mile fetch of water, open to the wind that creates the waves we are experiencing—steep and short, averaging one to two feet—just right for the new paddlers to get their sea legs. I watch Dan in the stern now paddling in unison with Tamara in the bow, working as a team. Midway across, the wind increases to a steady fifteen miles per hour with gusts to twenty. Nate guides us into the lee of a convenient islet for a rest stop.

Tamara, Dan, and Alan are discovering how their boats behave; they know what happens if you let your paddle catch the wind. (Strong winds can knock a paddle out of an unwary kayaker's hand, even knock the paddler(s) off balance and cause a capsize.) And Nate now has a better idea of how his people will react in similar conditions. Recharged, we head out on a different course—paddling off the wind, taking the waves at a forty-five-degree angle. As we build a comfortable rhythm, we must be making close to four knots. Smiles cross faces as "glory holes"—blue-sky breaks in the cloud cover—appear.

By late afternoon we have threaded our way out of the wind, well into the Granite Islands, stopping just short of the open ocean. A white shell beach between two unnamed islets looks like home. We land

and spread out to select tent sites, our stiff, soggy legs taking us into the forest of the larger northern islet and up a grassy slope. I find the remains of a sea lion, too far from shore to have gotten there on its own. But I see no sign of bears, just deer trails everywhere. I scout upwind, surrounded by the mottled grey trunks of coastal spruce, conscious of how few people have ever been here, conscious of the wind that once again threatens rain.

The Tlingit people of Chichagof believe the ravens are the official alarm clocks of all creatures. Two, perhaps three, ravens are calling now, in the half-light of dawn, well above the forest canopy. It is a call unlike anything I've ever heard: a melodious, metallic *plonk* like a raindrop striking a tin drum. From my sleeping bag I steal a glance out the tent— blue sky. Another look toward the distant kitchen down amongst the beach driftwood reveals life: Nate is making coffee and Alan stands atop the logs thinking about taking pictures. *Plonk.*

Today is magic. The sky stays blue and the sun warms us. Chichagof lies stretched out before us. Doolth Mountain is now but one of a series of peaks stretching from Sitka to Cross Sound. In the clear, smog-free air we can see sharp details of the 12,000-foot-high Fairweather Range emerging from the sea seventy-five miles in the distance.

We paddle on the rim of the Pacific, rising and falling in a world of liquid energy, riding the cobalt-blue backs of the great trans-Pacific swells. Our course runs parallel with the line of the waves that creates for us a world of peaks and valleys, our kayaks model ships in hurricane-sized seas. We stay within shouting distance as we watch one another drop out of sight behind an endless succession of waves. They come in sequences—most are perhaps fifteen feet high, but occasionally some are larger, menacing, so big they seem steep enough to break on us. For a moment, I sit in the trough, staring at the building wall of water that has traveled thousands of miles, rolling down on me, effortlessly lifting my kayak to the sky, and then rolling away—living its final moments before crashing against the continent.

By afternoon we've reached the Myriad Islands, moving back into calm, shallow passes and utterly still bays. Mimicking the stealth of Tlingit hunters, with our cameras Alan and I stalk deer feeding along the tideline. We glide smoothly through the shallows; seastars and sculpins slide beneath our keels as we take care not to go aground. By four o'clock we are island-camped again, boats and bodies angled into the sun atop a pebble beach in seventy-degree weather.

Our window of blue sky lasts through the following day—long enough for us to weave a ten-mile trail through the Myriad Islands and into Ogden Passage and Portlock Harbor. But this is the Alaska panhandle, where measurable precipitation is a near-daily occurrence. By the evening of the fifth day it is raining, and we are a picturesque group huddled beneath a free-standing, blue-and-white-striped tarp, looking for the world like an outdoor wedding reception gone awry.

Our awning is big enough to shelter our kitchen and ourselves, but it is sited well below the high tide line. Nate explains: "Bears. There are very few campsites on the mainland of Chichagof—usually only on the outwash plains of the salmon streams. There's not only not enough flat ground there, but also there's a good possibility of a bear visit. As long as we keep our kitchen within the intertidal where the water can wash away any scent of our meals, we minimize the chance of local bears associating this campsite with food."

Wise strategy. In my travels, I have encountered three so-called "problem" bears that frequently raid favorite sea kayaker camps. In the Queen Charlotte Islands, there's "Benjie" of Benjamin Point. The Glacier Bay National Monument rangers have a constant problem with bears becoming too familiar with campers and kayakers. With enough incident reports on a particular bear, the rangers will helicopter the offending animal into a less peopled region. In an extreme case the bear is shot, as was the case on Prince William Sound's Culross Island after a "garbage bear" began stalking people. We ask the obvious question of Nate: "Have you ever had a bear confrontation?" And we are relieved to hear him say, "No, Spirit Walker has never had anything beyond sightings."

Still, it's strange dining amidst the fucus. We now time our meals with the tidal rhythm—eating when the tide is low, day tripping or sleeping ashore when the tide is high.

It has been tough to return to rain; our energy just sags. The next morning, Nate has to nudge us along to break camp. We roll and stuff wet tents, and agonize over the incredible creeping damp that claims one sock after another. But once snug in our rain gear and paddling warm, our enthusiasm returns. We travel beneath the cloud-draped summits, past an oriental rainscape of wind-sculpted forests, spongy muskeg, steep cliff faces, and waterfalls plummeting to deep bays.

When we get to Dry Pass, the rain lightens. Nate pulls us over at the last protected beach before the open ocean, to scout the sea conditions outside. The same swells we had ridden so happily in the sunshine a few days before are grey and ominous today. Dry Pass is a tight opening to the outside, something we wouldn't take in any rougher weather or lower tide. Nate is jubilant; with calm seas by Alaska standards, we are going to make White Sulphur Hot Springs.

Yes, hot springs. It's all we can do to set the boats high up on the logs before we're on the trail to 104-degree bliss. The Forest Service maintains the springs and an adjacent cabin. We experience mixed emotions when we arrive. Other people are there: two kayakers all the way from Ketchikan and four folks in from Juneau on a floatplane. Some of us get a little shy, but introductions are made as we slip our naked bodies into the faintly sulphur-smelling pool, and conversations begin. We stay until we are nicely poached.

· GOING OUTSIDE ·

Nate is on edge during our last evening meal because of the changeable weather. He listens again to the Sitka NOAA weather forecast and says nothing. We have to be back on the lagoon side of Dry Pass for our floatplane pickup the next day, retracing yesterday's four miles of open ocean and lee shore, not to mention reentering the pass. Should it begin to blow, we'd be in trouble. A good kayak guide, Nate presents an alternative: we can portage through the forest to Sea Level Slough, where the Otter can land and meet us. Repetitive trips backpacking our gear and kayaks a mile distant sounds like work to us. We instantly begin offering little prayers to our personal weather gods, and the night stays calm. Alan and Nate take one last dip in the hot springs, and we depart White Sulphur, paddling to an unexpected sun rising through sparse clouds.

Alan and I jockey our kayaks for position as we move out through the protecting islets off the hot springs bay. Once through Caution Pass, we enter a large semicircular bay bathed in the delicate light of early morning. The sea's surface is windless, swathed in golden white spindrift. I rudder outboard of the two Nautiraids and paddle hard for position, turn, and grab for my camera. Alan and Nate pass close by, and Tamara and Dan are in the background—all framed by the exquisite sea-to-mountain setting of Chichagof. I focus, frame, and shoot until I finish the roll, and drift to a stop. My cameras are weightless as I enjoy the pleasure of having taken one of my best photographs. I fit a new roll, set the cameras back in their dry bag, and race to catch up. In the distant sky, way to the east, I hear the unmistakable drone of a radial engine.

THE KNIFE'S EDGE

The Queen Charlotte Islands

IF YOU WERE to kayak from the cities of the Pacific Northwest coast, beyond the margins of the last towns, beachfront homes, and marinas until only the forest and the sea lay off your bow, you would be tracing a course of a people who long ago paddled these waters.

From the Gulf of Alaska to the southern end of Puget Sound, these coasts were once the world to the Tlingit, Tsimshian, Haida, Bella Bella, Bella Coola, Kwakiutl, Westcoast, and Coast Salish. These first inhabitants of the Northwest Coast, like the coastal Eskimo and the Aleut of Alaska, were a sea people who created a culture built around the utility of a boat. Hewn from the massive red and yellow cedars, the dugout canoe of the Northwest Coast natives was their vehicle for hunting whales, fishing, traveling, and waging war. It was their vehicle in myth and legend. And now its spirit returns in a new form, the modern kayak, as a vehicle, a guide, and a teacher for a new people to find the ways of the past.

Graham
Island
BRITISH COLUMBIA

Masset

Hecate Strait

Queen Charlotte City Skidegate

Sandspit

Moresby Camp

Cumshewa Inlet
Skedans

Lost Islands

Windy Bay

Lyell Island

Burnaby Island

Dolomite Narrows

Rose Harbour

Ninstints

Kunghit Island

PACIFIC OCEAN

M o r e s b y   I s l a n d

N

· THE KNIFE'S EDGE ·

Choosing to travel by your own strength and skill, you can meet some of the challenges of the native paddlers. Suddenly you share the same wet dimension, the same pace and rhythm of the day, a common awareness of weather and distance, the ability to explore intricate coasts, and the intimate knowledge all of that brings. As you make the daily decisions of whether to paddle, when to camp, and where the bottom fishing might be good, you begin to feel a kinship with the natives who once called these waters home.

In time, as you journey farther from civilization as we know it, you may see the faint signs of the old civilization, one that flourished for over eight thousand years, poking out of the forest and along the beach, arousing your curiosity about these people who are famous for their totem poles and magnificent longhouses. And then one day you may enter a protected bay, land on a white shell beach beneath an unusual grass berm, and realize that this is not only a good campsite, but an old village site. You become aware that the depressions in the ground are the remains of the great cedar longhouses, and the berm beneath your feet is a midden—an accumulation of cast-off shells from centuries of ancient feasts.

If you find yourself trying to visualize the original village, asking what it was like to live here, wanting somehow to go back in time, to know the people of the cedar canoes, then you are ready to make the journey to the Queen Charlotte Islands.

Remote and unfamiliar, swept by the Pacific, separated from the British Columbia coast by a treacherously shallow fifty- to eighty-mile-wide strait, the Queen Charlotte Islands are a misty kingdom of islands and mountains, giant spruce and cedar forests, peregrine falcons and Steller's sea lions. They are, for their wildness alone, a sea kayaker's dream.

The Charlottes are a Canadian Galápagos, having the largest percentage of endemic plants, birds, mammals, and insects found anywhere in North America. The islands shelter great seabird rookeries, and are home to the world's largest black bears and to eleven species of whales. But it is the more than four hundred Haida archaeological sites that draw the kayaker to the Queen Charlottes, to paddle in the traces of the cedar canoes and wander through the deserted villages.

The Queen Charlottes' two major islands are distinctly different land forms: Graham to the north is relatively flat, with few offshore islands, and Moresby to the south is mountainous and hemmed with islands. Both islands' western coasts are victim to unpredictable and often violent Pacific storms. Because of these factors there is one favored route to kayak in the Charlottes—the southeast coast of Moresby Island.

Moresby is a one-hundred-mile-long island ridged with four-thousand-foot peaks that deflect and block the energy of the Pacific, sheltering the fjords and forested islands along its eastern shore. Few people live here; it is a true wilderness, and much of it has never been logged. The few mines have shut down, and the whaling station has rotted into its bay. The towns of the Charlottes—the Haida villages of Skidegate and Masset, the airport town called Sandspit, and Queen Charlotte City with its ferry route to the mainland—lie safely to the north. Only the loggers have threatened the nature of Moresby.

Over the past twenty years, a protracted battle to save the old-growth forests of Moresby has been waged by the Haida, local whites, and concerned environmentalists who blockaded operations to clearcut the island's entire forest. The world took notice, and the government of British Columbia grudgingly moved to establish the South Moresby National Park Reserve. In the end, the line was drawn at Lyell Island. To the north, thirty miles of Moresby's timber and most of Graham Island's trees will be clearcut. To the south for seventy miles, the one-thousand-year-old cedars, Sitka spruce, and western hemlock are safe: there are one thousand miles of wilderness seashore to paddle, with over one hundred emerald islands to visit without any clearcuts from beach to summit.

In the early summer, I join Steve Jones and John Eddy for two weeks of paddling the eastern edge of South Moresby. We stash our cars at Port Hardy on the northern tip of Vancouver Island, and as on the Alaska ferry, we carry our kayaks aboard. After arriving at Queen Charlotte City, we charter a converted salmon troller for a lift to the southern end of South Moresby, and disembark at a place called Rose Harbor, two hours paddling distance from Ninstints, the last ancient native village site still standing on the west coast of the Queen Charlottes.

Ninstints is the first of four places we will visit that retain the soul of this misty kingdom. The others are Dolomite Narrows, Lost Island, and Skedans. Like Ninstints, they perhaps best illustrate what influenced the Kunghit Haida to call their Queen Charlottes *Gaawa Hanas*, the "Place of Wonder."

〜〜〜

Ninstints was a town of twenty longhouses and more than three hundred people when smallpox came. Over a decade, family by family, house by house, the people died, until Ninstints was abandoned in 1875. The survivors fled to Skidegate, where remnant populations of all the stricken southern villages struggled to understand, to live, and to maintain their culture. By the turn of the century, the Haida had been decimated to one-tenth their original population. Ninstints was left open to the wind and weather.

Beyond the water's edge, rising above the beach grass, framed by a backdrop of encroaching evergreens stands a line of thirty totem poles. They are at least 130 years old, their weathered, silver-cedar faces mute: Bear Mother, Killer Whale, Sea Grizzly, and Cormorant stare out to sea in broad, bold relief. These carved forms of both natural and supernatural creatures are symbols and signs of ownership, called crests, that represent the wealth and power of the family that lives in their shadow. The setting, the experience of paddling beneath their ageless stares, still convey that power. We too are silent.

I walk up onto a natural terrace and into an intricate web of ancestral memories, sacred sites, and complex myths beyond my imagination. I drift silently among the totems and walk the perimeter of the long-house depressions. Cloudy House was home to the "Striped Town People." Mountain House sheltered "Those Born in the Southern Part of the Islands." And at the south end of the bayfront, the large forty-six-foot by forty-nine-foot Thunder-Rolls-upon-It House once stood, where the last chief, Ninstints, and his people, "Those Born up the Inlet," lived and died.

The Haida named everything—every house, reef, mountain, and rocky beach—not simply to assign a place-name but to integrate each entity into a belief structure that was passed from generation to generation. Often varying from family to family or village to village, their legends offered explanations for a world in which the sky at night sometimes blazed, the salmon swam to their feet, and men sometimes paddled from this cove never to be seen again.

George F. MacDonald, in his beautiful ethnography *Haida Monumental Art: Villages of the Queen Charlotte Islands*, described the world as perceived by the Haida:

> *To the Haida, their world was like the edge of a knife cutting between the depths of the sea, which to them symbolized the under-world, and the forested mountainside, which marked the transition to the upper world. Perhaps because of their precarious position, they embellished the narrow human zone of their villages with a profusion*

of boldly carved monuments and brightly painted emblems signifying their identity. Throughout their villages these representations of the creatures of the upper and lower worlds presented a balanced statement of the forces of the universe.

The view from among the totems passes over our kayaks and out through the cove's entry. I realize that where I stand, listening to the wind and measuring the whitecaps across the channel, I've found the best vista from the terrace, the point where whether to go fishing must have been discussed from time immemorial. For a moment our kayaks become cedar dugout canoes, imaginary children run naked across the pebbles, there are songs from the row of longhouses mixed with the garrulous voices of ravens in the treetops. For a moment I'm there, in prehistory, in Ninstints.

A new urgency in the wind, backing to the southeast, brings me to the present. We cannot stay on the island; it is sacred to the Haida, maintained by them, and since 1983 watched over by a resident caretaker. We linger as long as we can and then slip quietly out of the bay late in the afternoon.

∼∼∼

The day is fair and windless, deep in the protection of Moresby's mountains. The descending hillsides mirror themselves on the water of Dolomite Narrows, our bow-waves the only disturbance, our paddles making the only sound. Through the reflection of a clear blue sky, the bottom comes up to meet us. Wisps of kelly-green seaweed part to reveal mats of seastars, like an oriental carpet of rich colors—royal purples, coral reds, sky blues, and sea greens—all cruising about on thousands of tiny tube feet.

It is a bed of unexpected intensity, the sea life so concentrated, so plentiful, draped across the sea floor in what appears to be a backwater. But as we paddle farther in, the backwater becomes a tight pass three hundred yards long, separating South Moresby from Burnaby Island to the east. Through it, the daily ebb and flow of phytoplankton-rich seawater squeezes north then south and back again, the current supporting the filter feeders. The entire intertidal is layer upon layer of expired butter clams. Over all, rock and spider crabs, turban snails, and starfish scuttle, fully conscious of our presence. Grounding ashore, I set my boots down between starfish, and the abandoned shells crumble with my weight.

Beyond the tideline, a deer grazes along a grassy bench that was once Narrow Strait village, one of three known settlements within an arrow's flight of the passage. Like many of the old village sites, Narrow Strait village has a parklike lawn between the sea and the forest. Deer, introduced to the island in the 1920s, gravitated to these open spaces created by village sites and have pruned any sapling that dared break ground ever since. We set up camp on the grass as the tide ebbs. The pass empties like the biblical Red Sea, the sunset highlighting random arcs of clam squirts.

∿∿

Why is it that so many epics begin with "we got a late start"? It must have been 10:00 A.M. when we left camp, a small unnamed village site just east of Dodge Point on Lyell Island. John and Steve take an inside route, bound for the well-preserved longhouse foundations of Tanu village. I am captivated by the low silhouette of Lost Island, the most isolated island of the Charlottes, four and a half miles into Hecate Strait. We part company, planning to meet two days hence.

The weather is questionable, whitecaps are visible off the point, and the sky beyond is a sullen grey. As I clear the headland, doubt begins to creep in with the spray. *Xe-u´*, the southeast wind spirit, is bringing rainy, tempestuous weather. Two miles out, I find myself in a steady twenty knots with four- to five-foot following seas about fifty feet apart. I'm soaked but warm enough and feeling strong; with each stroke my kayak strides across the grey seascape. Through a rain shower, I can barely see the island.

From beneath my hood I scan my surroundings, gaining a collective picture of wind, waves, greys, and greens in motion. A seabird is working upwind in my direction, using the shelter of the swell, disappearing in the trough, then rising and dumping wind at the crests. I watch with increasing fascination as it struggles toward me. When the bird is about thirty feet away, I realize it is a common murre bent with the wind, barely making headway. It does not see me. We drop into the same trough. Twenty feet, ten feet, right to my bow—wings flare in alarm. A tiny astonished eye holds mine for an instant, and we part abruptly.

I'm dazzled by the fact that we almost collided. A wave comes aboard, startling me, bringing me back to the wet present. I stroke hard to come back on course. The murre didn't see me because the wind is getting stronger, and the seas are building. I start to watch the wave train running up my starboard stern quarter. The significant waves, the one or two largest of a set of seven to ten waves known as a train, are now five to seven feet high and breaking. I turn to meet them, my paddle knifing their backsides.

I have been out no more than forty minutes when I turn and go with the train toward the shelter of Lost Island. Each wave builds behind me, raising my stern, almost sending my kayak rushing forward if it were not for my quick, chopping back-paddles to check the boat from surfing. Wave by wave, I approach the south side of the island—a windblown set of sea stacks with small forests in its cracks and draws. I recall that the chart showed a small cove that now becomes visible ahead. I pass the outer reefs, curl right, and paddle into flat, protected water.

I let out a triumphant yell: *AaaaaaaaROOOOH.* Two startled bald eagles guarding their nest natter at my announced arrival. Steller's sea lions on the inner rocks not more than forty feet off my bow don't show any interest in budging. I turn right toward a boulder beach, certain the sea lions haven't seen anyone here in years. They watch as I get out and stand, and then they bolt for the protection of the deep. They know man after all.

I turn toward higher ground, searching for a campsite, my mind on getting dry and making hot soup. I am relaxed and elated. Beneath the low, prickly needles of a spruce is a clearing strewn with flotsam—space for a tent and shelter for my stove. The wind howls beyond the bay. I look out at my boat with affection and the growing awareness that I'd been very lucky.

~~~

Like many of the villages, Skedans is on a tombolo—a spit connecting a small island to a larger landmass with bays on either side. Skedans has a fine bay opening to the south. The twenty-six longhouses that once covered the spit faced the bay above a pebble beach. All that remains of them today are the depressions marking the individual house pits. Fifteen totem poles stand, lean, or lie throughout the village. Nearly all are mortuary poles—the legacy of sudden disease and the world's museums' preference for taking the taller and more elaborate house frontal poles.

Mortuary totems, about fifteen to twenty feet high, are carved with symbols that speak of the transition between worlds. In a cavity at the top were placed the remains of the house chief, and a painted front plaque acted as an epitaph. Near the center of the village is one such mortuary pole that has fallen toward the bay. Beside it, lying on the forest floor, is a skull sweatered with a delicate green moss. At first, approaching it from behind, I think it is a rounded rock. Then I see the eye sockets, the unmistakable shape of a human head. I stare at that skull, bone from a man that lived here over a hundred years ago, bone now so beautifully taken in by the nature of decay, as if being kept warm. Not without reverence, I take a picture and move away.

Still seeking spirits, I climb a promontory overlooking the village, again a vista for many ancient eyes, to sit and read, take some notes, and soak up some sun. A small black bear, perhaps a yearling, breaks from the forest at the far end of the bay, an intense blackness ambling along the beach. During my climb, I had come across the remains of a deer carcass and the depression left by a much larger bear who had fed continuously on the meat, leaving its scat in seven neat piles in a radial arc. I'm definitely going to hang the food bag at this campsite.

I watch the young bear nosing for food through the tideline piles of matted kelp. It will not see or smell me, and I am in no hurry to gain the beach. We go on about our separate interests until the noise of a Zodiac rounding the tombolo startles both of us. The bear hightails it and I step back into the cover of the forest, noting that we both had the same reaction to the arrival of people. A party of seven, a non-native guide and six tourists, lands and fans out to explore.

I have not seen my partners for two days, and we had not seen anyone else since Rose Harbor; in time I work my way down the slope and into the village to say howdy. I encounter a scene of quiet embarrassment. One of the tourists has been caught secreting the skull in her knapsack, a memento of her trip to the Queen Charlottes. The guide is ashen; he has carefully replaced the skull in its bed of duff, and says to me if that skull had been stolen, the Haida tribal council might revoke his right to bring tourists to the villages. I'm troubled by the woman's indignation at being refused her "trophy." I mention the bear, and the group edges toward the Zodiac and away.

~~~

Steve and John paddle into Skedans not much later, and we camp away from the village for the night. Our final day, an eighteen-mile slog into a grey, wet, moderate wind, takes us from Skedans up Cumshewa Inlet. With each stroke of the paddle, we are bringing to a close a trip into the prehistory of our coast that will haunt us for a lifetime. For the past fifteen days we have lived in the eddies of a culture so remarkable, it lives on in spirit not just throughout the glades of the abandoned villages, but in the reemerging culture of the Haida and within us as well.

The inlet is heavily logged and enclosed. At its head lies Moresby Camp, once a major booming yard, now home to a few homesteaders. The landing is littered with logging machinery and choker cable rusting in the rain, adding little to the bittersweet end of our trip. We are to be met by a man from Sandspit with a trailer for the boats and a case of "high-test" beer. But we aren't quite sure what day it is. Our man is nowhere to be seen. We stand around looking at our watches, momentarily captive to both the spirits of the land and the timetables from another world.

ORCA

Johnstone Strait to Blackfish Sound

THEY COME OUT of the North Pacific depths in a coordinated attack. Orcas, the killer whales, quietly encircle the sockeye returning to the rivers of British Columbia. The salmon mill in confusion as the orcas, one by one, charge the center of the school. Those salmon prudent enough to flee discover the ring of orcas, like a net holding them in, each predator patiently awaiting its turn to feed.

It is early summer off the northwestern tip of Vancouver Island. The scent of the Fraser, western Canada's largest river, draws the salmon on as they follow their spawning urge, seeking their ancestral stream. They gather and turn south into the increasingly confining waters of Queen Charlotte Strait. The orcas follow, feeding at will.

By June, families, or pods, of orcas begin arriving at their summer "village." This gathering site is at the western entrance to a great passage of saltwater that continually floods and ebbs between the massive northern flank of Vancouver Island and the myriad islets and inlets that buffer the mainland of British Columbia. Known as Johnstone Strait, this entrance is one to three miles wide, forty-seven miles long, and over one thousand feet deep. It is a natural gauntlet the salmon must run to find their spawning grounds. During the five months the salmon pass this way, up to 170 blackfish, as orcas are also known, will

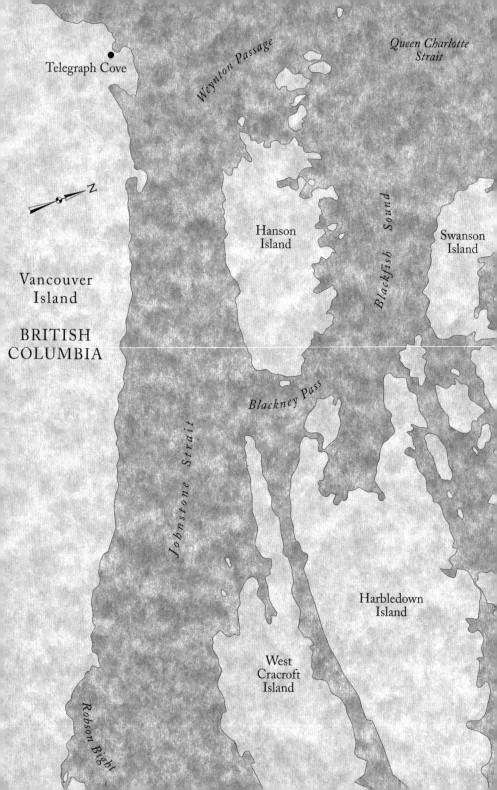

Telegraph Cove

Weynton Passage

Queen Charlotte
Strait

N

Hanson
Island

Blackfish Sound

Swanson
Island

Vancouver
Island

BRITISH
COLUMBIA

Blackney Pass

Johnstone Strait

Harbledown
Island

West
Cracroft
Island

Robson Bight

congregate in these waters, herding salmon, teaching their children, families reuniting with families.

So too in June the humans come, heading north from the universities and research centers, passing through Seattle and Vancouver up the fabled Inside Passage to Johnstone. They bring with them underwater microphones, cameras, and computers. They bring, as well, a curious reverence for the orca that separates them from their brethren. For they have a common conviction that the orcas are something greater than one more precious organism swimming in the sea. They study the behavior of a marine mammal that rules the world's oceans and has captured the hearts of all who study it. Paul Spong, who initially approached studying the orcas as you would a laboratory rat, described in 1974 after six years of research a far different understanding:

> [The orca is] an incredibly powerful and capable creature, exquisitely self-controlled and aware of the world around it, a being possessed of a zest for life and a healthy sense of humor, and moreover, a remarkable fondness for and an interest in humans.

This viewpoint was not easily accepted. The orcas had long been named killer whales—toothed whales that have no enemies and, in Dr. Spong's estimation, no fear. They have been witnessed by seafarers to be swift and effective hunters of all major fish and mammal stocks. The orcas themselves were hunted sporadically by the Japanese and the Norwegians, and shot at by every self-righteous fisherman out for the same catch. They were assumed to be ruthless, voracious killers. The assumption was wrong.

Into the 1970s, in both Canada and the United States, researchers' fascination with orcas and other whales resulted in a groping realization of these marine mammals' remarkable abilities. The first studies were conducted with captive dolphins, porpoises, and beginning in 1969, orcas, often in the circus atmosphere of the new marinelands. The first tests were simple nose-the-proper-button-and-receive-half-a-herring physiological studies. But in Paul Spong's visual acuity research, something went marvelously wrong: after twenty-four hundred half-herrings and a ninety-percent success rate, Skana, the first captive orca to be studied, began giving the incorrect answer time after time—her only way to tell the researcher, "I want a new game."

Skana continued the education of Paul Spong, at one time seeming to correct him for leaving off a pectoral fin on her portrait by pointedly wheeling about her pool, the omitted fin splashing the artist. On another, Skana slashed her teeth across Paul's bare feet, only touching and causing no pain. He recoiled in instinctive fright but returned his foot to the original position. Skana repeated the movement, her head rising out of the quiet pool, her teeth sweeping over his extended toes. Again Paul flinched, but being a dedicated experimental psychologist, he repeatedly dangled his foot. Each time, Skana would lunge until he controlled his involuntary reaction. Skana then stopped and vocalized, staring back at Paul from the middle of the pool. He then realized that she was intentionally deconditioning his fear of her, establishing a bond of trust.

Through the 1970s, the studies of orcas evolved. No one doubted the whales' intelligence; their gentleness and family loyalty turned public opinion into a love affair, yet no one really knew the orca. Dr. Spong began studying free as opposed to captive orcas in 1974, by establishing a research station on uninhabited Hanson Island at the northern entrance to Johnstone Strait. Taping their voices and monitoring their daily patterns in the tidal wilderness, Paul's research turned personal and public. Together with a growing family of researchers, film teams, writers, and musicians, the clinician became an advocate and a voice for the orca, and Johnstone Strait rippled to the wakes of kayakers, researchers, and orcas interacting in open curiosity.

In 1981, David Arcese had caught wind of Dr. Spong's studies and asked me to join him on a kayak trip to Johnstone Strait. Quiet, soft-spoken, fascinated by whales, David's curiosity about orcas must have rivaled Spong's. We were well into September, late for seeing orcas, but going anyway, as we car-topped our kayaks along Highway One north through the clearcuts and gentle peaks of interior Vancouver Island.

Our put-in was Telegraph Cove, a tiny, protected bay rimmed by second-growth evergreens. Along the back bayshore lay an exhausted timber mill whose saws had been stilled for a decade, a general store and a boat launch for the new economy of sport fishing, and a board-walk connecting an unplanned string of sturdy fir-framed houses. With one green exception, these houses were painted white, roofed with corrugated tin, and each was well kept and lived in. They were sited along the tideline wedged between outcrops of granite and the stumps of long-gone old growth. Spartan, clean, dotted with the passing of ravens, Telegraph Cove was as it once was, hedged in by the landform, overlooked, blessed to grow no bigger.

We paid the store owner a small sum for launching privileges, and paddled out into Johnstone and a rising southeasterly. Hoping to be with orcas and intent on making Robson Bight eleven miles distant, we headed east hugging the Vancouver Island shore, our paddles feathered to knife the wind.

This first paddle to Robson would be a stormy one. Much of our time was spent grounded beneath a rain tarp, as a strong southeasterly tore up the strait. We saw only two orcas pass on our third day. The following morning, wet and cold, we packed and paddled back to Telegraph Cove, promising to return.

~~~

Robson Bight is not quite a bay—it is a bend in the shoreline, an indentation deep enough to warrant a name but too exposed to give a vessel safe anchorage. In the years following our paddle to Robson, the bight would gain the attention of the world for its unique orca visitations. It would also narrowly miss becoming a timber booming yard, where the great log rafts would be created and towed to market. And its uplands, the climax forests of the Tsitika River valley—the last virgin watershed on the 285-mile-long island—would be slated for clearcutting. The government of British Columbia would designate the bight a marine ecological preserve in 1982, but in the end the timber industries have been allowed to cut the valley and only a 200-foot coastal buffer has been saved.

There were other changes: new paths and new attitudes were bringing new people to the water's edge. Each year another massive ocean liner joined the popular cruise ships sailing the Inside Passage. Two or three ships a day passed the bight, immersing thousands of tourists into the magic of the forested islands, the eagles overhead, and, if they were lucky, the orcas. Telegraph Cove's old tug *Gikumi* had been converted to an orca-watching vessel, breathing new life into the Telegraph Cove economy. But one phenomenon stands out in the decade of growing interest over the orcas of Johnstone Strait: sea kayakers. These were newcomers with a relatively gentle impact, silently tracking to Robson Bight.

On a Sunday in July 1989, I returned to Johnstone Strait to meet up with David, who had founded Northern Lights Expeditions and was beginning his seventh season guiding sea kayakers into the strait. Amidst the salmon fishermen and whale watchers, we load and launch our group of twelve new kayakers into the little-changed harbor of Telegraph Cove. The weather is overcast and dry as we paddle out through the port entrance, the new seafarers bumping gunwales, hurtling this way and that as they learn to steer the fast, stable double kayaks. David and his assistant guide, Steffie Ackroyd, are moving like sheepdogs through the little flock, instructing and reassuring the neophyte kayakers, as we enter the open waters of Johnstone Strait.

As each pair of paddlers gets a rhythm going, we begin to speed up, relax, and take in our surroundings. Behind us hills of conifers rise up into the low clouds, hiding the steep three-thousand-foot almost-mountains that crowd the northern shore of Vancouver. Before us, two miles of open water sweep away to the east and west to form the strait. Beyond the crossing lies Paul Spong's Hanson Island, one of a hundred low-lying islands to explore.

With the chart and a firsthand look at this landscape, I can realize, almost see, the forces that have shaped the scene before us. Off our bows, miles inland, the islands turn to mainland and rise to mountains, like a mirror image of Vancouver Island. Between these two natural barriers a millennium of glaciers has come and gone, rounding the islands' edges, mining channels as deep as fifteen hundred feet along the strait.

As we approach Hanson Island, David steers us toward Weynton Passage and the entrance to Blackfish Sound. We cheat as only a kayaker can, and paddle behind the tiny islets that rim the west end of the island, avoiding the main channel and the beginning of the opposing flood tide surging in from the Pacific.

Once through the pass, we stretch out into the open waters of Blackfish Sound, moving at a beginner's pace. This is a casual exploration; all of us are watching for orcas, some more impatient than others. David is in no hurry. After all his summers running trips along the strait, he knows the people in his charge will settle into enjoying all there is to see and do here—and see orcas.

David is good at this business, in part because he respects the spirit of the land as well as the orcas. He knows the locals and works with the Kwakiutl people of the region to protect their heritage sites. He is respected by the long-term researchers who help him set self-imposed guidelines on kayaking in the presence of whales. And he knows the orcas from his reading, attending conferences, and simply being here in contact.

In a few days, we'll move back across Johnstone to the camps north of Robson Bight where whale sightings are routine. For now, we get to know our kayaks and our partners as we paddle our way to camp.

We beach on a small pocket bay that faces south and set to unloading the boats and putting up tents. I wander through the kitchen and discover it is possible to snitch a fresh piece of cornbread. As our dinner of fresh salad and grilled cod, salmon, and crab disappears, we idly watch the evening go by. On the far side of our vista, the last of the salmon fishermen power back to Telegraph, the whine of their outboards fading toward the setting sun. A bald eagle soars off to the left, over a perfect little island. For many of the people on this expedition, this is their first day in company with eagles. Conversation stills as we watch the great scavenger wheel away.

One of our group asks David about the small minke whale we'd seen earlier in the afternoon, when suddenly the ground begins to vibrate, strongly enough to stop the conversation. An ocean liner, massive and at speed, enters Blackney Pass southbound, passing our camp about a half-mile out. The light shines from the ship's cabins with the color of a campfire. I can almost imagine the disco music over the sound of the engines. Although we're close enough to see people, the decks are empty. The ship swings to ride the centerline of the thousand-yard channel, comes around to port, steadies up on a course down Johnstone, and is gone. We stay quiet for a bit, to ruminate over this remarkable visitor. Elegant to some, an extravagance to others? No one says. We are undeniably on a different cruise.

The following days we explore Blackfish Sound, trailed by shy yet curious seals. Our real intent shows in our scanning of the way ahead for telltale dorsal fins, our ears tuned to the distant whoosh of orca breath. On the morning of our fourth day, we move our camp five and a half miles to the Vancouver Island side of Johnstone Strait for some serious orca watching. No sooner have we established camp than David spots a pod well out in the channel. We assist each other with our boats, and one by one we paddle from shore to intercept.

Whale watching is not unlike the behavior of a professional sports photographer on the sidelines of a football game. With every play, he moves farther downfield in an attempt to predict the advance of the team. The key to this analogy is that he cannot enter the field. Neither can we. Placing boats across the oncoming path of an orca pod might disrupt their activity—feeding, sleeping, playing—causing an unknown amount of stress to an already too popular mammal.

We paddle fast and hard, angling to approach the whales' course well ahead of them. David calls a halt and we gather into a group, staying still and hoping for the best. We wait. David had said that orcas have a distinctive cruising pattern of deep diving for three or four minutes at a time, then a series of shallow dives of ten to fifteen seconds duration. If we're in the right place, the pod should begin a shallow diving sequence about two hundred yards off our bows. We wait and watch, necks swiveling left-right-left, fingers focusing lenses from thirty feet to infinity and back.

"They're behind us!" someone shouts, as the sudden sound of exhaling air reaches us across the water. We turn to face the pod. The whales surface again, and we do a sort of sotto-voce mutual squeal because they have turned, coming straight at us. At a hundred yards, the orcas dive again and we go quiet, darting glances at each other. David says, "Just stay put."

One by one, their dorsal fins rise into the air right in front of us—so close it looks like a sure collision. At less than thirty feet, the largest bull aims right for me. I know from my reading and David's assurances that orcas do not intentionally attack or even bump kayakers in such a nonthreatening situation. I'm just trying to focus my camera. They dive, the male's six-foot dorsal fin sinking with a subtle side-to-side movement and I realize it's flexible, not knifelike, not a weapon. I look into the depths of mid-channel for the passing of the twenty-five-foot-long submarine shape, its dorsal fin faint in the watery darkness—five tons of *Orcinus orca* beneath my fifty-five-pound kayak.

We watch transfixed as the pod swims beneath us, their white-to-grey "saddles" across their backs marking their progress. The orcas make one final surface, each exhaling followed by a sharp intake of air, and then they deep dive, tails rising from the water with an unhurried, fluid motion.

The water surrounding our kayaks ripples from sudden displacement. No one lifts a paddle. David suggests a course we can follow and we begin to move north toward Weynton Passage, keeping to the right of the pod's probable path.

In David's opinion, this pod is asleep. "Orcas sleep on the move, the adults taking turns on watch. See how they all breathe in unison." The pod surfaces well to our right, in easy rhythm, exhaling in the same uncanny synchronism; their high, jet-black dorsal fins rise and fall, parting the clear, jade-green water in mid-nap.

We learn that these four whales are called the C-5 subpod, a part of C pod, one of the larger resident families that summer in Johnstone

Strait. The leader is C-5, the matriarch, the fifty-eight-year-old mother of C-2, a big dorsal-finned thirty-two-year-old male; C-10, an eighteen-year-old female; and C-13, a five-year-old toddler with the characteristic hook-shaped baby fin. These whales will stay together for life, a life that nearly matches ours in longevity.

Their colorless titles are disturbing—we would name them differently. David tells us that the numeric designations are a necessity for scientists. Whales in early studies were identified by more distinctive monikers—Wavy, Saddle, Nicola—with each name identifying a particular physical feature of the individual whale. But that became unworkable with the discovery of so many more whales at Johnstone.

Our own "pod" of fourteen kayakers looks pretty professional, paddling easily. Mirrored in the reflective greens and greys of the strait, our paddles rise and fall in unison, bow and stern sailors intent on the whales. Though David rarely shows it, he is pleased with the trip. We have achieved the skills to safely travel these waters, the people have warmed to the land's character, we all have been doing our dishes, and now we are in the company of orcas.

Suddenly the orcas' cruising pattern changes. They have doubled their speed, coming farther out of the water, awake and excited. The orcas have picked up echolocations from H pod, infrequent visitors to this area, moving through Weynton Passage and headed our way.

We paddle hard to keep up, but fall far behind as the giant mammals surge up the strait to greet their friends. The first orca breaches, his full body leaving the water, a ten-thousand-pound silhouette on the horizon, then a mammoth splash. Other orcas are "spyhopping" or swimming in place, propelling their upper torso clear of the water to see around them. Still others below are most likely curling around neighbors in physical touch. The sounds they are no doubt making underwater—clicks, whistles, and screeches—are identifications and greetings. Another whale breaches, this time close enough for us to see the distinctive markings of the whale's white and black stomach.

David brings us to a halt well short of the melee, at a two-hundred-yard distance, grouped, watching. Gradually the hubbub dies, and we lower our cameras. The pods deep dive, showing their tail flukes, and minutes later they surface separated. The H pod continues with the tide along the east side of the strait, and C-5 subpod crosses back toward our camp.

We have had our close encounter. In the gathering dusk, C-5 and her family swim away, and we slow to a stop to watch them go. Clustered together, our paddles resting across our neighbors' boats, we try to verbalize the sensation of paddling with orcas, David every bit as animated as the rest. But words are insufficient. One by one, our paddles bite the still waters of Johnstone Strait for the Vancouver shore.

POINT OF
CONTACT

◆

Nootka Sound

EIGHT A.M. Gold River, Muchalat Inlet, the west coast of Vancouver Island. The *Uchuck III* lists as her crew hoists a one-ton truck from the town pier into her forward hold. Surrounding the ship's hatch lie pallets of groceries, coiled wire, and tool boxes bound for the logging camps out near the coast. Alongside, boom boats shove and bump log rafts toward a shoreside paper mill. The air is fragrant with wood smoke, the fjord hazy in the morning sun.

The mate gestures for us to begin loading our six kayaks on the main deck, aft of the hold. My Polaris slides in behind Ross Anderson's old Escape on the sunny starboard side. The engines below rumble into life and go slow-astern. The *Uchuck* works on her springline and then comes ahead, entering the inlet, bound for Nootka Sound.

The ship gathers way on a westerly course, tiny in the immense geography of the inlet. Muchalat is fourteen miles long and less than a mile wide, bounded by three-thousand-foot-high forest walls plunging another fifteen hundred feet to its silted fjord floor. Midway down the arm the sun has gained the ridge, and we bring full cups of coffee up to

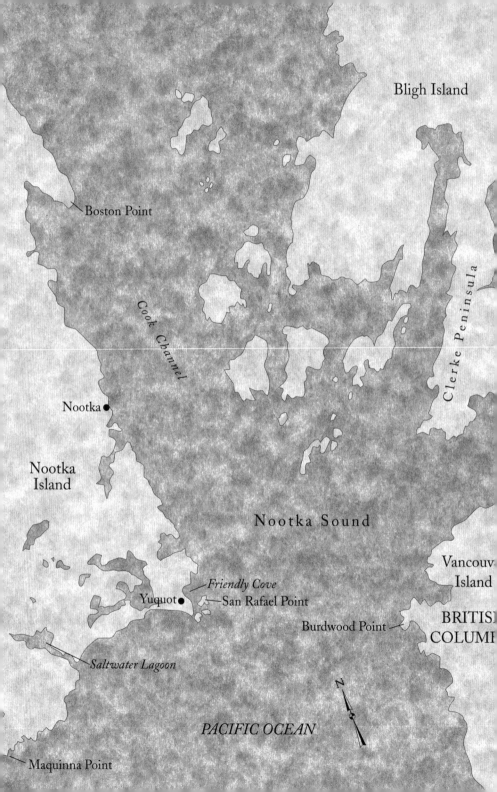

Bligh Island

Boston Point

Cook Channel

Clerke Peninsula

Nootka •

Nootka
Island

Nootka Sound

Vancouv
Island

Friendly Cove
Yuquot • San Rafael Point

Burdwood Point

BRITISH
COLUMB

Saltwater Lagoon

N

PACIFIC OCEAN

Maquinna Point

the stern rail. Shoulder to shoulder, we watch the *Uchuck*'s brilliant white wake purl away, subsiding to racing blue-velvet waves that widen toward the dark-green hillsides.

The *Uchuck III*, a ship with the ironic Westcoast native name meaning "calm waters," is one of the last remaining coastal freighters on the West Coast. Once a World War II minesweeper, the 136-foot-long, twenty-four-and-a-half-foot-wide, fir-hulled ship cuts a living out of the inlets and fjords of western Vancouver Island, supplying the loggers and fishermen between Gold River and Tahsis. But, of importance, the *Uchuck III* also quite literally drops off sea kayakers.

By noon we're approaching the western shore of Nootka Sound. The captain yells down at us to bring our kayaks forward to a point beneath the booms. I slip into my fully loaded kayak, and the deckhands fit two slings forward and aft of my cockpit, the ship's winch engine revs, the booms creak, and I'm lifted above the leeward rail to the applause of my companions. With a smooth motion, the mate handling the winch swings me outboard—about twenty feet in the air—and gently lowers me into Nootka Sound.

I unfold the chart and lay it across the coaming. Ross Anderson comes alongside and holds a corner of the map into the wind. We orient the map and locate our position: we're in about 336 feet of water about one hundred yards off Boston Point, a good four miles from the Pacific Ocean.

Though the water is reasonably flat, the afternoon winds are strong enough to force us to paddle close to the shore, traveling south into the sun. Ahead of us the hills that rim the sound begin to taper off, forming low-lying coastal plains that extend out of our sight as Point Estevan on the south and Bajo Point to the west. Together they form a broad bay that hourglasses in from the Pacific creating an entrance to Nootka Sound. We aim for the western side of this opening and the old summer

Indian village known as Yuquot. Bligh Island, Cook Channel, Boston Point—our historical pulses quicken as we paddle the shore of Nootka Island. We're only a few miles from sharing a goal that began for both of us years ago.

My father was a sea captain; I was raised around ships, enamored with sea stories, voyagers, and passages to discovery. I've read every oceangoing book from Hollings Clancy Hollings's *Paddle to the Sea* to Joseph Conrad's *Typhoon*. I worked every ship I could, from longlining on halibut boats to reefing the topsails of the replica of Sir Francis Drake's *Golden Hinde*.

So too, Ross, throughout his life and career as a writer and reporter for *The Seattle Times*, has gathered multifarious bits of history, exploration, and discovery, culminating in his purchase of an original French bootleg copy of Captain James Cook's *Chart of the Coast of America*. "I've always loved cartography, maps, and charts," he says. "I happened to come by one of Cook's original charts of the North Pacific from his exploration of 1779. The only place marked from San Francisco to Prince William Sound and Cook Inlet was Nootka Sound. For twenty to twenty-five years that was the only chart of the North Pacific, and Nootka became the only port on the Northwest Coast, a port almost unknown two hundred years later."

The latitude of Nootka Sound is 49° 35' 30". It is the latitude that Spanish explorer Juan José Perez Hernández would plot one August day in 1774, the latitude that would be the destination for Captain James Cook and his midshipmen George Vancouver and William Bligh. It is the latitude at which the European seafarers came in contact with the natives, ushering in the era of the sea otter trade.

Nootka Sound became what historians call the point of contact for the Northwest Coast. Over the next twenty-five years, more than two hundred ships would drop anchor in what became known as Friendly

· POINT OF CONTACT ·

Cove. Long before the Columbia River and Puget Sound were known, the Spanish, English, and Americans refitted ships here, grew gardens here, and vied for the sovereignty of this forested, deep-water wilderness.

Yuquot: the name is derived from *yukwitte*, to "blow with the wind." Prior to the arrival of the Europeans, it was the spring and summer residence of the Moachaht people—one of twenty interrelated tribes known as the Westcoast people, originally named Nootka by the European explorers, that live on the outer coast of Vancouver Island and Washington's Olympic Peninsula. At the point of contact, thirteen families from seven Tahsis Inlet winter villages summered here.

The first people of Nootka Sound lived a life that one could envy. The men set out for whales and fished for halibut, salmon, and cod. The women gathered berries, camas, and tiger lily bulbs, dried surf grass and sea grass into cakes for the winter, and collected the bountiful clams and mussels whose shells were tossed just outside.

Today Yuquot is overrun with brambles. From the crescent beach, paths break through the rampant vegetation and go up onto the old midden. The soil beneath is eighteen feet deep, composed of shells and fire ash, the detritus from at least four thousand summers past.

The old village site is on a triangular spit that leaves the forest and runs flat and windswept to a series of rock outcrops and islets jutting out into the sea. On one side, a beach of small stones and scarred drift logs stretches westward for a mile against the force of the Pacific. On the other side lies the shelter of Friendly Cove. In the center is an old school yard with tumbledown goalposts, the school deserted and open to the weather. Across the grass, the substantial but empty church of Pope Pius V thrusts its spire toward the sun. Facing the cove, a north-south line of five small, boxy frame houses mimics the old plank house sites, their backs to the wind and sea. They too are abandoned, except for the new two-story, big-windowed home of Ray Williams and family.

· THE HIDDEN COAST ·

Ray is the Westcoast people's caretaker of Yuquot. A big man with a broad, playful face, he looks strong and young though he is probably fifty. He fills the chair propped up against the front of the house, facing the sweep of the cove. As a young granddaughter's dark eyes peer out at me from the protection of the doorframe, Ray and I talk over a fee for our party to camp down the beach.

When Ray talks he uses short, slow, soft-toned sentences rich with the old language sounds: the *kw*, *tl*, and *sh*. We talk about the weather, the winters here, and we dicker on the price of our stay. I photograph his son's carved cedar masks and Ray himself. He tells me of the move by the government to make Yuquot and Friendly Cove a historical park commemorating the arrival of the Europeans. The Westcoast people weren't too enamored with the idea. "It wasn't a great day in our history," he says.

An outboard surges to life with a roar, and Ray's friends in from town run it briefly to make sure a repair will take. With the din, our conversation dies; Ray and his friends are going hunting. I've got dinner to cook. We settle on a nominal fee for our campsite and shake hands, as the engine starves and the sounds of the wind and the surf return.

The government did manage to place a rock cairn out on the last point with a plaque commemorating the negotiations between Cook's onetime midshipman Captain George Vancouver and Spain's envoy Juan Francisco de la Bodega y Quadra. These negotiations became the Nootka Convention of 1792, a political sally toward the eventual British sovereignty of the region. The Westcoast people were never included in the resolutions. Fifty years after contact, the sea otter were hunted out and the ships departed, leaving European diseases, alcohol, firearms, laws, and religion to a bewildered and weakened Westcoast people. Their ancestral lands were taken, rights to freely fish their rivers removed, and Friendly Cove—too remote for Europeans—became uninhabitable to the Moachaht. All that remains today are the Ray Williams family and a plaque.

~~~

Dinner brings a discussion. We have three days to explore, but as a group we have different aims and abilities. We decide that Friendly Cove will be our base camp. From this location, we can slip outside for trips up and down the coast. And if the weather worsens we can paddle inside, exploring the islands of the sound.

In the morning, a north wind and clear sky draws three of us out, Tom Schwartz, Karl Weatherly, and me. Rounding the point and heading west along the beach, we paddle fast, enjoying the freedom of our boats that are now empty of camping gear.

The sport of sea kayaking has an exuberance that derives from an intermingling of the sea's natural energy, the paddlers' strength, and the fluid movement of the craft. Watching my friends meet the ocean, their kayaks bursting through the waves, I can see their exhilaration. Taking water over my own bow, my sunglasses speckled with salt spray, I turn my attention to the route ahead, enjoying our ability to explore outside the protection of the cove.

We paddle around the rocky point, and meet a cross sea of low swells, wind-driven chop, and waves rebounding from the rocks. The result is a confused pattern of waves running in all directions. At times these errant energies meet and collide to form a momentary column of water known as a pinnacle wave. You don't really know you're on a pinnacle until you're suddenly rising up, higher than any wave yet encountered. While you're still rising, the waves just as suddenly continue on their respective courses, for the moment leaving you high and dry. I look over at Tom just as a pinnacle wave tosses him airborne, his paddle frozen in mid-stroke. He looks down where the wave had been, and his kayak returns, smacking the sea with a light-boat "thwomp."

A submerged rock surfaces ahead, and I brake with a quick paddle stroke, surprised that I hadn't seen the reef earlier. We circle the danger and slowly negotiate the rock garden off Maquinna Point. The wind is increasing and the sea is getting rough, so we turn back to a small cove where the mouth of a tidal stream leads inland to a saltwater lagoon. As we approach the outflow, we watch the surf breaking to our right along the beach to Yuquot. I'm not that accomplished at surfing in a kayak and still get butterflies on approaches like this. But the small headland on our left juts out enough to force the swell to refract around it and lose its punch.

One by one, we ride the dwindling surf into the cove. The forest of the headland blocks the wind and shades the stream. A sand beach borders the outflow, stretching toward Yuquot. Beyond lies a short, winding river. I pole my boat with my paddle through the shallows into deeper water, cedar water, water turned the color of tea by the oils of the wood. Overhanging firs are mirrored in the windless passage. Two mergansers, a green-headed drake and a reddish-brown hen, leave the upstream bank for the water, reluctant to fly. With each twist of the river the forest recedes, replaced by beds of salt grass. The channel broadens and turns into a shallow lake a third of a mile across. We paddle silently, a seemingly instinctive reaction to the sudden change from boisterous ocean to tranquil lake. In the morning this lagoon would host browsing deer, river otters, herons, and perhaps black bear. At midday it's quiet—just the mergansers shuffling along the reedy water's edge, getting some distance from these strangers.

The next day, we study the chart. The coast south of Yuquot looks even more formidable, westward facing and exposed to the full power of the prevailing swells. You can almost see the way the coast catches the wave action, the land pushed back, the weak strata eroded into small bays and even smaller coves. The stronger rocks remain as reefs and islets that act as a barrier, dissipating the sea's energy off-shore. Between the reefs and the shoreline lies an avenue for safe kayaking and the potential for exploration on beaches seldom seen by contemporary man.

The crossing from Yuquot is two miles; the weather is calm and a mid-sky stratus sucks the color out of our surroundings. The sea surface looks oily and reflective, bulging with a long, lazy swell. I shoot a few frames of Tom and Karl, knowing the pictures may never be published; picture editors almost never choose a grey-day image. But grey weather is the other fifty percent of summer on the western coast of Vancouver Island, and we've learned to enjoy it.

Upon reaching Burdwood Point, we turn south and steer our kayaks into the backwaters of the reefs. One by one, we enter a maze of narrow passages alternately flooding with seawater and then ebbing to reveal a wainscoting of purple and orange sea stars. Squeezing our kayaks into little reef and rock enclosures, we find ourselves in a private aquarium carpeted with sea urchins and anemones and overlaid with bull kelp bulbs and fronds. Shoreward, the environment changes to little bays unaffected by the moderate swell. We ghost in, disturbing the kingfishers, noting potential campsites for another time.

Crossing back, the tide carries us through the entrance to Nootka Sound. The light on the point marks Friendly Cove and the promise of a campfire and friends. As so often happens in sea kayaking, I have no desire to head home. Looking back over my shoulder to the entrance, I wish that we were traveling for the summer, running on the outside when weather permits, working our way along the coast from sound to sound, and taking shelter in places like Friendly Cove. For Nootka is but one of a series of sounds that penetrate Vancouver Island's exposed Pacific coast.

· THE HIDDEN COAST ·

To the south lies Barkley Sound, a popular kayak destination. Part of Pacific Rim National Park, it is known for its Broken Islands, a pristine island group with a sliding scale of kayak experiences from quiet backwaters to the rough-and-ready front edge of the Pacific. North from Barkley, past the towns of Ucluelet and Tofino, lies Clayoquot Sound. Sea kayakers come here for the offshore islands of Blunden and Bartlett and the outside run to the fun of Hot Springs Cove. North of Nootka, connected by Tahsis Inlet, is Esperanza Inlet, the center of extensive logging activity. North again is Kyuquot, more wild than any of the sounds. This inlet leads outside to the Bunsby Islands, sea otters, and the "experts only" Brooks Peninsula.

Tomorrow we paddle to meet the *Uchuck III*. We will go back up Cook Channel to Gold River, and return to our own winter villages, to our own history. I grip my paddle and stroke to catch up with my friends. We skim the rocks at the entrance to Friendly Cove and paddle the last strokes toward a waiting fire.

SOUTH FORK

◆

The Skagit River Estuary

OF WEBS AND CYCLES, zones and edges, methylotrophs and polychaete worms. From salmon fry to sticklebacks, bulrushes to willows. Harriers, hawks and, in winter, eagles high in the cottonwoods. Beaver, deer, and coyote live here, and if the freeway were not a barrier, black bear. These are ingredients of the Skagit River estuary—a salt marsh, a detrital soup, a rich stew of life rhythms percolating beyond the dairy farms and the distant hum of the human day-to-day.

The Skagit is a Washington river, born tumbling from the eight-thousand-foot glacial cirques of the North Cascade mountains, coursing down the steep, U-shaped valleys, flowing west. Growing with tributaries—the Cascade, Sauk, and Baker rivers—the combined flow swells to a volume greater than the Colorado before it leaves the foothills for its alluvial plain.

Unfettered by mountains, the Skagit curls and turns, meandering through one hundred thousand acres of rich farmland. The plain is famous for tulips, peas, and cauliflower. It is flat as a pancake except for a few isolated, curious hills, once islands, marooned by the ten-thousand-year continuous advance of the river's estuary.

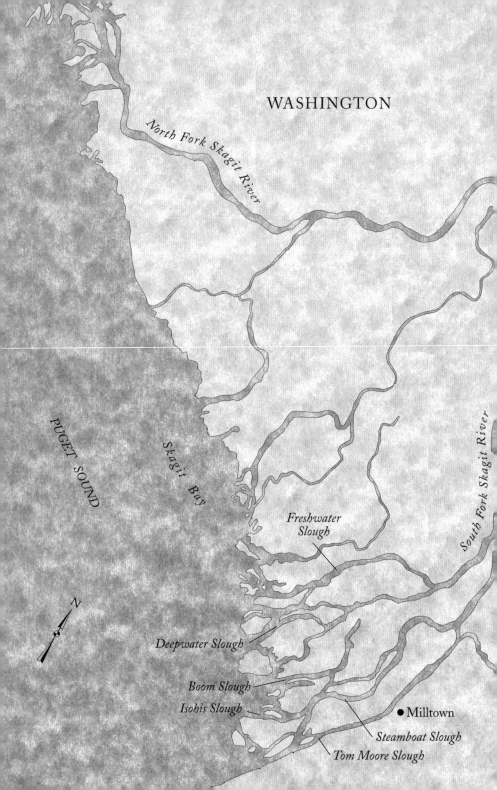

WASHINGTON

North Fork Skagit River

PUGET SOUND

Skagit Bay

South Fork Skagit River

Freshwater
Slough

N

Deepwater Slough

Boom Slough

Isohis Slough

● Milltown

Steamboat Slough

Tom Moore Slough

· SOUTH FORK ·

Below the farm town of Mount Vernon, the Skagit divides into two channels—the North Fork, which transports its silt quickly west, intent on surrounding Ika and Goat Islands, and the South Fork, the lesser flow, which moves at a sleepier pace, branching into sloughs named Freshwater, Tom Moore, and Steamboat to build the estuary.

Milltown once was a small, bustling South Fork river stop in the logging and steamboat days of the late nineteenth century. Today it is just two houses, a population of four, numerous barn swallows and, on the river side of the dike, a State Game Department boat launch.

The Skagit swirls and eddies into the launching area with the energy of spring. It is a good time to come, an early April afternoon. The alder and willow are blushing, taking on color, and the cottonwood buds perfume the slough with a honeylike fragrance. I roll my sleeves above the elbows and shove my kayak, loaded for the weekend, into the current. While setting my spray skirt, I drift past a fleet of low, flat, plywood duck boats painted olive drab, stacked atop the floats below Ella's daffodil-lined river cabin.

"Did you see her hands?!" old neighbor Tronsdal had said about Ella once, not unkindly. She does have big hands—hands that remain a symbol of the strength and size of this woman's life. Ella had toiled alongside her husband, shore logging (making up rafts of stray timber to sell) in the 1930s, and trolling for salmon—always connected to the water, the river. In her mid-eighties, shrunk by age and the world around her, she lives alone, alongside Tom Moore Slough, with her diminutive Chihuahua that wears a little knitted vest and shivers as a way of life.

A few duck boats are missing from the last float, evidence that Slicker and always Ziegler, who might love this place more than all of us combined, have gone into their duck cabins for the weekend. I've suspected for years that these men could give a damn about ducks or duck season. I think they, like I, now come just to be out here.

Kayaking the Skagit, and estuaries in general, is unlike any other sea kayaking experience. I think of it as nature's nursery school for fledgling kayakers. Safe, shallow, and sandy-bottomed for the most part, the water is slow and manageable, except during the winter rains and spring runoff. Estuaries also offer lessons in discovery. The sloughs are narrow and interlacing, bending and turning, creating a sense of adventure and curiosity about where each passage goes. Above all, the estuary teaches the kayaker about a habitat of profound richness. Acre for acre, the estuary is the most productive of our environments, busy with the transit of marsh hawks, the darting of baby flounder, the shufflings of muskrats—activities that the inquisitive kayaker is privileged to observe.

Knowing the tidal rhythms allows the paddler to use the energy of the tide to advantage. The tide table for this day in the southern Puget Sound region looks like this:

April 3   Tuesday   Southern Puget Sound Tides

HIGH Tides		LOW Tides	
1:24AM 10.9ft	**12:03PM 8.9ft**	6:57AM 7.3ft	**6:39PM 0.4ft**

(For the Skagit estuary, which is north of this region, the correction is plus twenty-seven minutes for high tide and plus thirty-eight minutes for low.)

Ideally, if you put in at Milltown on a morning outgoing ebb tide, you have a free ride to the bay. Explore all day, and enjoy the two- to three-mile-per-hour returning flood to the landing. Today's tide is not a free ride but not so extreme as to leave me stranded. Over the years, I've experienced the many tidal variations, from thirteen-foot storm tides that inundate everything in the estuary, to minus-two-foot low tides that leave the tideflats bare for miles into Skagit Bay, prompting the vivid term "sand prairies."

◄◄ *Brash ice, low clouds, tide-water glaciers. Water dominates the land at Barry Arm, Prince William Sound.* ▲▲ *In the lingering spring twilight of Alaska, kayaks are tethered for the night on Copper Bay, Knight Island.* ▲ *Spring and the oil spill assessment teams return to the Bay of Isles, one winter after the Exxon Valdez oil spill.* ► *First to shake the burden of snow, an islet on the north shore of Port Wells greens in the midday sun.*

▲ *Paddling through a mirror image, sea kayakers pass beneath the mountains rising out of Copper Bay, north coast of Knight Island.*

▲ The clarity of Alaska's light and the patterns of sea foam play to the photographer off White Sulphur Hot Springs. ▼ Port, strut, and wing of the De Havilland Otter frame the leading edge of islands off Chichagof's west coast. ▼► Mesmerized, Alan and Nate watch the motions of a jellyfish near the ruins of a Doolth Mountain gold mine. ► On a hot, low-tide afternoon, fucus frames a sea star in the protected lagoons inside Dry Pass.

◄◄ *Roof stringers of solid cedar logs, twenty-five inches in diameter and forty-five feet in length, lie fallen across the central common room and family terraces of "House that is Always Shaking" at Ninstints.*
◄▼ *Bear, thunderbird, and orca in carved cedar— Haida mortuary totems stand at Ninstints, imposing in decay.* ◄ *Time in resonance—a grass blade snipped by a feeding deer, a human skull fallen from its mortuary totem and covered by a filigree of moss—past and present together at Skedans village.*
▼ *Everywhere there are the subtle movements of small fish and crabs, and more subtle still the creep of snails and starfish for those patient enough to spend an afternoon drifting through Dolomite Narrows.*

▲ *Orcas eye-to-eye. While feeding, the whales of A-12 subpod surface and resurface among kayakers in Blackfish Sound.*

▲ ▲ *The mainland side of Johnstone Strait becomes a maze of narrow passes. The tide will transport you deep into a myriad of islands and six hours later flush you back out with memories of village sites, kingfishers, and a hermit's offering of fresh fish.* ▲ ◄ *Kayaker-friendly bull kelp, a sign of deep water near reefs undulates beneath the surface of Johnstone Strait.* ▲ *Sheltered from the wind and anchored by kelp, a kayaker stretches in the sun after a visit to Robson Bight.* ► *Log-boom chains rust on the shore at Telegraph Cove. It is morning and the forecast promises good weather: clouds but no rain, fifty-five degrees Fahrenheit, with winds from the north at five knots.*

▲ *Along the south side of Nootka Sound's Bligh Island is a small, magic beach where the sand stretches out beneath clear water to suspend kayaks as if in mid-air.*

▲▲ *Aboard the* Uchuck
III, *Mary Rothschild smiles
with apprehension before the
winches lift her over the side
into Nootka Sound.* ▲ *A
contemporary (1927) totem,
crowned with the returning
forest, stands to the sunset at
Yuquot.* ◄ *A father's pride
in the skill and artistry of his
son's carvings shows in the
face of Ray Williams.
Yuquot, Nootka Island.*

◄ *A July sunset on Clayoquot Sound, Vancouver Island, British Columbia.*
► *After falling asleep in the summer sun, I awake with a companion—* Thamnophis ordinoides—*the Northwestern garter snake.* ▼ *On a foggy morning, one greater yellowlegs among a pack of dunlin feeds between patches of last year's bullrushes.*
►► *At the confluence of Steamboat and Boom Sloughs, behind a line of alders and past a beaver lodge there is a backwater slough that hides ducklings and salmon fry.*

· SOUTH FORK ·

To learn the river, to know the pathways of the estuary—which passages cut through, which ones go dry at any given tide—you have to become a Skagit-scale Mark Twain. The topographic maps for the estuary lack the necessary detail, and local knowledge is too specific or too general. There's no way to learn this marsh other than putting in and letting the current take you down.

I paddle mid-channel of Tom Moore Slough, between banks lined with overhanging alder and groves of towering cottonwood. The river is cold and quiet, a moss-to-mud color, steadily flowing toward Skagit Bay and Puget Sound. My eyes scan the surface for snags, the banks for change, signs, or critters. A dusty Wonder Bread wrapper hangs impaled on an alder branch about fifteen feet above the water, evidence of how high the winter floods crest.

I am alone on the river. Aside from my duck cabin friends, about a mile down Tom Moore, these sloughs see only an occasional trolling fisherman, and duck season in the fall makes this place too dangerous for kayakers.

Water sounds. Something moves quickly; a river otter or muskrat, maybe a beaver, hides in the undercut bank. I slack my paddling and drift, folding my arms over my paddle shaft. On this early spring day, I can sense the marsh holding its breath as it gears up for a season of growth—the latent energy still in the ground, the sun, and the instinct of migrations.

About three hundred yards below Milltown, on the right, a side slough cuts hard back and runs northwest. Newcomers wouldn't take this channel, especially with a tide as low as this afternoon's. But if you're a kayaker or canoeist, it's good to know it goes through from Tom Moore to Steamboat slough and the heart of the estuary.

I begin my turn early as the current sweeps me past; I paddle hard to swing around and up the stream. The waterway is shallow, at times forcing me to pole off the bottom and dodge sunken logs. For a third of a mile, I paddle and push my way against the current, my eyes level with the lip of the bank, layered mud, and exposed roots. The skunk cabbage is about a foot high but still just shoots, its leaves and flowers tucked and enfolded like sleeping bats. Winter grasses are faded blond, and last year's spirea, once so fragrant, like pink lemonade in bloom, has dried to a dark rust.

This part of the estuary is known to biologists as the woody-stem zone of the salt marsh. It is the high ground, the least salty and more diverse in plant life. Its drainage sloughs are lined with a fine, deep, dark, bacterial mud packed with microscopic life. Its banks and bogs are habitat to bittern, coyote, and deer. Exiting this nameless connecting slough, shallow water gives way to the deeper channels of Steamboat, and I run with the river.

Camping in the Skagit estuary is illegal unless you have permission from land owners like Slicker or Ziegler. Even then there is little high ground to use. Years ago I began caretaking an old duck cabin on the west bank of Steamboat, where I hole up for the night. I check the chimney for bird nests and retire early for tomorrow's paddle.

April 4   Wednesday   Southern Puget Sound Tides

HIGH Tides		LOW Tides	
2:24AM 11.1ft	**12:53PM 8.5ft**	8:21AM 6.3ft	**7:49PM 1.0ft**

Sea kayaking is a sport of many bags: a camera bag inside a rolltop dry bag, a big lens bag of the same type, a food bag, a clothes bag, a day bag, in addition to the rest of the gear—tripod, water bottle, and my Eternal Thermos—just to go picture-taking in a kayak at dawn. At six o'clock in the morning, I'm feeling particularly courageous. Everything froze last night; my kayak is candy-coated with ice. My gloves are poor excuses for pogies, and my past few breaths hang around me like tiny cumulus clouds. All bags packed, I slide the boat off the high bank and, balancing between kayak and shore, plop onto my cherished Thermarest cushion. Dragging my muddy boots in the current to wash them off, I slip them dripping into the kayak.

At forty minutes before sunrise, the surrounding estuary is a near-colorless tapestry of blue-blacks. Only an aura of lavender light over the Cascade peaks hints of dawn. Thrushes, wrens, and sparrows paint the darkness with their morning song, oblivious to my silent passage. I drift with the tide, keeping my body motionless while the outgoing current sucks me into Boom Slough. A riffle ahead marks the remains of an old steamboat, its keel and flat ribs coated with river silt. I drift safely by and into an open pondlike enclosure, listening to the birds, the drips and gurgles of the upland marsh, and the gnawing of the resident beavers.

I rudder toward the sounds, and in the half-light spot two mature beavers feeding along the slough edge. When they see me, they take to the water, their great tails slapping the surface in noisy defense. The disturbance brings the eerie sound of approaching wing beats, as a great horned owl, white feathers against the dawn sky, flares above me and then arcs away in the heavy morning air.

In the west, the sun line descends, pink hues chasing the retreating night. I decide I'd better hurry if I want to reach the bay before sunup. Below the woody-stem zone, the forty-foot-wide slough is lined with winter-tattered cattail. About every sixty feet or so, a long-billed marsh wren in the early stages of nest-building stops to give warning at my passing. From the mouths of joining sloughs, pairs of mallards and mergansers explode into flight, and great blue herons en route to the bay silently veer around me and continue on to their choice fishing spots.

As the cattails and marsh wrens thin out, I paddle into a zone of braided channels and low sand banks peppered with tiny, yellow salt grass spikes. The change of scene from one of cattail corridors to sand prairies gives the sky a physical dominance. Overflights of snow geese and tight flocks of dunlin move above the margin of the bay.

The most visual and vocal of the Skagit's winter residents, the ten thousand pairs of "snows," as the snow geese are known, are one unusual, positive result of bad logging practices. Over the past 150 years, so much timber has been cut in the Skagit drainage that the resulting hillside erosion has dramatically increased the size of the estuary. The added sediment load created sand prairies and a perfect environment for salt grasses, primarily the three-square bulrush, a preferred food of the snow geese. With the growth of the three-square, around 1880, so the old farmers say, the first flock of approximately two hundred snow geese wintered in the Skagit.

The snows are beautiful birds, about the size of the Canada goose but a golden white with black wingtips. They fly in Vs, heading inland to spend the day feeding in the farm fields and returning to the estuary at dusk for a night roost. In a week, this pattern will begin changing with the rapid growth of the salt grass. Then the snows will feed on the prairies—waddling lawnmowers snipping the fast-growing salt grass shoots, fattening up for the two-thousand-mile May migration to Siberia, to nest and rear their goslings.

The sun is nearly cresting the mountains as I run out of estuary. Before me are Skagit Bay and Puget Sound swathed in a thin, low fog. Seemingly at the edge of the earth, I turn back and ground up on a salt grass bank. The tide is still on the ebb. I extricate my booted feet from the kayak and slowly roll to a standing posture. There is no cover out here: I stand in six inches of water that stretches away to infinity. Though I keep my movement to a minimum while I set up the tripod and mount the big 600-millimeter lens, the creatures around me are subtly distancing themselves from this vaguely hunter-like apparition.

A harbor seal leaves first. A heron flies and lands out of gun range. The last small flock of geese honks away. But I know from experience one species will stay.

Dunlin are sandpiper-like shorebirds about the size of a fluffed-up robin on stilts. Like the snow geese, they are gregarious during migration and fly in large, dense flocks. Words can't begin to describe what goes on out here in the morning, at sunrise, when the dunlin take to the air. With synchronized flock movements, they take on the shape of a great, diaphanous amoeba undulating above the estuarine mud. At forty miles an hour, turning in unison, they reflect the first rays of sun.

Dunlin feed with the outgoing tide, skittering from one newly exposed mudbank to another, poking and probing their two-inch beaks into the mud for amphipods—the small crustaceans, twenty thousand to a cubic yard, that thrive off the nutrients of the salt marsh.

A flock wings over to my lobe of earth and I begin to frame them, using the horizontal bands of last year's bulrush stalks for composition. As the fat dunlin hunt and peck, through my viewscreen they look like a musical score, a series of whole notes wandering purposely through a staff of bulrush set in the golden reflection of sunrise. Approaching to within twenty feet of me, the closest veer away, threatened, yet anxious to follow the receding tide and continue feeding. A sudden alarm-peep, and they're up and gathering more and more birds into a mass of feathers in flight across the surface of the bay.

My salt grass bank suddenly devoid of dunlin, I'm down to amphipods—not my preferred photographic subject. I pack my cameras, relieved by the respite from shooting into the dazzling sun. I've been out here for three hours and the ebb tide has long since stranded me. Not for the first time, I drag my kayak over the flats to the Boom Slough channel for the paddle back to Milltown and the hum of the human day-to-day.

SHI SHI

♦

The Olympic Peninsula Seashore

UNLIKE OREGON AND CALIFORNIA, Washington is not known for its dramatic shoreline. From the Columbia River north to the native fishing village of La Push, the coast is a 135-mile, more or less flat, wide beach, embayed at Gray's Harbor and Willapa, forested here and summer-homed there. But once past La Push, the topography begins to rise. Passing Cape Alava, the coast geology changes from recent Quaternary glacial and alluvial gravels, sands, and silts to the thirty-five-million-year-old marine sedimentary and volcanic layers. These strata, some soft, others hard, have been compressed, faulted, and inverted, and today, along the northwest edge of the Olympic Peninsula, the folded layers dip steeply northward to meet the force of the Pacific in an exposed cross section.

This northern corner of Washington's seacoast is made up of forty miles of storm-bound bays and high-cliffed headlands. Here there are scalloped, sandy beaches separated by sea stacks and arches so spectacular they are a surprise after the uniformity of points south, so intriguing they draw sea kayakers to dare the surf and storm in order to paddle through the rugged colonnades and camp on the deserted expanses.

In late July, the weather around Seattle had stayed hot long enough for Glen Sims and me to plan, pack, and drive to the coast. West of

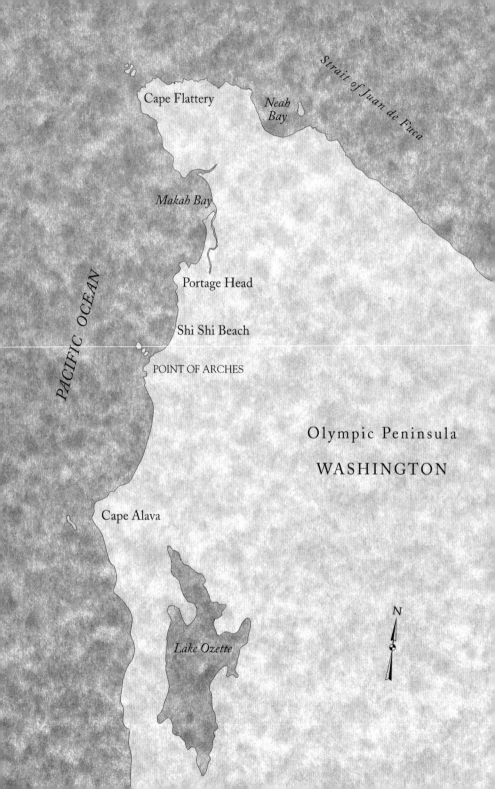

· SHI SHI ·

Port Angeles, we take State Highway 112 along the top of the Olympic Peninsula to Neah Bay and the ancestral lands of the Makah Indians, or "Outside Coast People." Following a dwindling set of dirt roads, we pull to a stop at Makah Bay near the mouth of the Sooes River. The surf is running from three to five feet. Once our kayaks are loaded, we time our paddle out so that we miss the larger waves and enter the Pacific.

Sims. Every time we paddle, at some point his melodious baritone booms across the water, like oil upon the seas of introspective thought, startling the scaups and in general lightening the mood of the moment. Glen Sims has a beautiful voice and is a strong kayaker; he still loyally paddles an old rootbeer-colored, scratched, and mended Mariner Escape. With Sims I can expect fast paddling, bizarre meals—the result of one-stop shopping along the road—and if the timing's right, an old ballad.

When first I came to Liverpool
I went upon a spree.
Me money, alas, I spent it fast,
got drunk as drunk could be.
And when me money it was all gone,
it was then I wanted more.
But a man must be blind to make up his mind
to go to sea once more.

Our destination is the Point of Arches and Shi Shi Beach, once a Makah summer village site, now included in the primitive area of Olympic National Park. Shi Shi (pronounced shy-shy) is a beach of mythic character, a northwest Shangri-La of golden sand framed by natural spires and majestic arches that act as collectors of the curious, seekers, and free spirits.

In the early 1970s, the consummate nonconformist Freedom and his wives, Sund the poet and Sybil the good witch, and others, packed in their wood-burning stoves and joss sticks over the old logging road to live on Shi Shi. They built whimsical driftwood cabins and lived freely in company with the negative ions. Today, they and their cabins have gone with the coming of time and the National Park Service, but Shi Shi remains the same—no road, no facilities. It is just as it was: mystical, beautiful, and wild.

I first visited Shi Shi in 1975, packing a full Kelty three miles over what is still, even in the driest August, the muddiest trail in the Northwest. I had checked and planned for low tides, and learned from a chance meeting with one of the Shi Shi people that I should leave the path early. In through the forest and down to a small bay, I then continued south from Portage Head alongside the crash of the Pacific. Teetering over the wave-cut benches, slogging through the soft sand edges of the beach, I sweated my way toward my first glimpse of Shi Shi.

If sweat is a main ingredient in the journey to all great places, I am glistening, living proof of Shi Shi's greatness. Fifteen years later, I vividly remember that first moment. I cleared my eyes, brushed back my wet hair, and saw a cavernous hole in the shaded wall of the headland. I walked into its cool darkness and entered a chamber created by the sea—a three-legged arch with Shi Shi beach framed in one passage, the Point of Arches visible through another. A wave surged into the grotto and I stepped back, waited, and then quick-stepped out into the sunlight.

Most every year since, I have made my way to Shi Shi, once on a lonely Christmas, another time in hot August when everyone on the beach went nude. Somehow, each visit is as fulfilling as the first, despite the collapse of the three-legged arch, the grandest entrance one could imagine to a Northwest wonderland.

· SHI SHI ·

Well he booked me on to a whaling ship,
  bound for the Arctic seas.
Where the ice and snow and the cold winds blow,
  Jamaica rum would freeze.
And the worst affair was I had no gear,
  I lost all me money on shore.
It's then that I wish that I was dead
  so I'd go to sea no more.

Our good weather has dissolved to a grey and threatening seascape off Makah Bay. Glen and I turn to each other with rueful expressions: we can always paddle back here if the beaches south prove too rough. But one hour later, it's back to blue skies and good moods, as we pass the old fallen arch and stand off the north end of Shi Shi. Surf is hitting the beach hard, appearing to be six to eight feet high and breaking steeply—too much for us. We paddle south along the beach, looking for a calmer entry, watching the backs of the waves attacking the beach.

Closer to the Point of Arches, the east-southeast swell is blocked by the point's mass, rebounding through sea stacks. We ride into the beach on a perfect three-foot, slow-breaking surf. My favorite campsite is along the upper edge of the shore where the beach meets the coastal forest—it lies deserted. Glen and I carry the kayaks above the tideline and set our tent among the bleached drift logs.

The beauty of this campsite is its closeness to the point and its distance from the other campers. From our camp, Shi Shi stretches two miles north in an unbroken curve. With a sharp eye we can spot little clots of hikers arriving fresh from the trail, big with packs, larger than life in the shimmering midday heat. When they reach the beach they discover the backpacker's exquisite agony: sand. One by one, groups valiantly head our direction, only to fall short, lumbering into the driftlogs to find a site, set up a shade tarp, and massage their aching calves. Once they've set up camp, they continue toward us—barefoot, halter-topped, carrying cameras, holding hands—moving toward the point.

Come to the Point of Arches when the tide is low, when the sea stacks and islets are accessible. At low tide, the sand has filled in around the bases of the arches and stacks with a wave-ribbed floor, creating a sort of yellow brick road. There are arches to pass under, ramps to climb, and caves to amplify the sound of the surf. Rock corridors, their high walls hung with sagging starfish, lead off into tight passages. A turn one way may dead-end at a dark, secret tidepool; another leads to a spray-struck Pacific vista. We watch the couples, the solitary strollers, one by one approach the edge of the stacks and disappear within until the evening tide flushes the explorers back up the beach to their camps.

> *Sometimes we're catching whales me boys,*
> *and sometimes catching none.*
> *With a twenty-foot oar I'll stroke it around*
> *till two o'clock in the morn.*
> *And when the evening shadow falls*
> *we'll rest our weary oars.*
> *It's then that I wish that I was dead*
> *or safe with a girl on shore.*

At 5:15 the next morning, our camp is enveloped in a light fog. Glen starts the stove and puts the coffee on to brew, while we carry our kayaks down toward the misty sea stacks. Within the hour, we paddle out day-tripping south to Cape Alava and the ancient Makah village of Ozette, long ago buried by a mud slide and today a valued archaeological site. By noon the day blossoms, making our return hot and windless—good picture weather. I shoot a great roll of the sea stacks, and I'm ecstatic as we return to camp.

About a half hour before sunset, we paddle into a small bay on the south side of the Point of Arches formed by flanking forest-topped sea stacks. Glen moves toward a "hole in the wall" arch piercing the base of one stack, to see if we can run it. We really like paddling through arches. Our pattern has been to sit off the arch, safely beyond the rocky shore, observing the wave patterns curl around the sea stacks and watching for sunken rocks to emerge as the bigger swells subside beneath the arch. If it's deep enough, calm enough, and clear on the other side, we run it. I drift toward shore, changing film, stopping once to paddle a few strokes away from the wavebreak, and drift again to secure my spray skirt. Then comes a shout.

I can't hear what Glen is saying; I just get a sense of the surprise and alarm in his voice. I look up from my camera and into the face of the largest wave I've seen all day. It is suddenly, instantly silent as the wave steepens, blocking the noise of the surf. The sun penetrates the wave, making it translucent. Glen, twenty feet out, is lucky enough to be pointing seaward, and with one swift stroke he drops behind the advancing wave. I am not going to get off that easy: I'm pointing obliquely toward a rock-strewn bench, with no headway, a Nikon draped around my neck. I have time for one decision, two strokes, a desperate sweep, and I'm rising up on the wave's shoulder, my Polaris's bow batted back, broaching—parallel to the breaking wave. I lean into the foam, and catch a glimpse of my camera leaning with me. My paddle finds the back of the crest and anchors me. The soft chine of the kayak begins to slide along the front of the wave as I hang atop. I'm suddenly in control, rushing shoreward at fifteen miles an hour, buffeted in the welter of the wave.

I try to turn the boat, using the paddle to pull the bow back over the crest, but I can't. My head snaps back to where I'm going: rocks, a jumble of oddly uniform washer-dryer–sized rocks. But I'm rushing above them, maybe six feet above them, the foot of the wave filling in, flooding the reef just ahead. A rock larger than the rest breaks into my peripheral vision, and I visualize what my boat will do if I tag it. I involuntarily shut my eyes, and my kayak passes over.

The wave is five feet high now and slowing. I redouble my efforts to pull the kayak back over the crest. I think, "I'm going to make it." I lean way out and pull the blade toward me again without losing the fulcrum that has kept me atop the breaker. Before I can bump bottom, I gain the backside and sprint to deeper water. All I can do is laugh and shake. The wave that captured me may have been a rogue wave, a statistical probability stalking the world's oceans, according to marine weather expert K. E. Lilly, Jr.:

> *Waves on the ocean are made up of a large number of different waves having various heights, periods, and wave lengths. It is not surprising to find that waves occasionally reinforce each other, creating unusually high and steep waves compared to those prevailing around the area. In a storm-tossed sea, such waves will appear seemingly out of nowhere, roll ominously along for a few minutes, and then disappear.*

Though I would be hard-pressed to call my sleeper wave a rogue, it very likely developed in the same way.

Waves are simple enough in definition. What intrigues me is their quality of surprise. Perhaps the essence of going to sea, whether aboard a 200,000-ton ship or a fifty-five-pound sea kayak, is that the mariner is at the mercy of the capricious power of the oceans.

· SHI SHI ·

To paddle the coast edge well, to extend one's paddling horizons to the world's oceans, the kayaker has to learn the sea as well as any mariner. This is the sustaining joy to sea kayaking—to really learn the ways of the ocean, to become capable of handling a variety of seas, winds, and anomalies like rogue waves.

I learned a good lesson. I had failed to pay attention to the outer swells, and I'd been too close to the shore break. But I had ridden that wave, and brought the boat and me back. Without looking, I know my camera is totaled. Purely as a formality, I place it beneath my spray skirt. Still I'm elated, soaring with the experience.

Glen and I come together, and he recounts that the last he saw of me my bow was high in the air. His memory of the shoreside rocks plunged him into the scenario, "How do I retrieve the body?" For a few moments our conversation dies.

We paddle out around the sea stack, the arch forgotten. As we approach camp, we check over our shoulders for the wave train and catch a little one into Shi Shi.

Come all you bold seafaring men,
   come listen to my song.
When you come in from those long, long trips,
   I'd have you's not go wrong.
Take my advice, don't drink strong drink
   or go sleeping with no whore.
Get married instead and spend all night in bed
   and don't go to sea no more.

EMBAYMENTS

Willapa, Coos, and San Francisco Bays

THE PACIFIC COAST is indented with bays, and better for it. They provide shelter from the relentless wind and sea, and they lend a sense of permanence—though perhaps an illusion—to a land in rapid transition. Bays are odd in their attraction—passive certainly, so quiet they tend to be overlooked. While the headlands and capes have tourist overlooks and the great crash and bang of the surf, the bays usually have a heron or two in patient reflection and little towns backed up against the bordering hills. Willapa Bay in Washington and Coos Bay in Oregon are like that. San Francisco Bay was once that way, too. I've come to like these and other bays. They offer special kayak explorations into the backwaters of the land and sea.

WILLAPA BAY: Ordered Hosts

Virginia Graves looks mortified. Surrounded by the weathered artifacts of the Pacific County Museum, she protests my suggestion that I start my story with her casual reference to Willapa Bay's fifty square miles of mud. "I should never have told you that. Besides, we call them tideflats—fifty square miles of tideflats—you just can't call it mud." Virginia is a striking woman, tall and graceful, somewhere in her seventies. She came right out of her chair when I mentioned I was

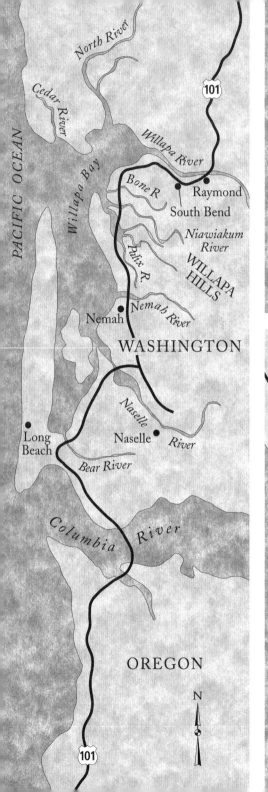

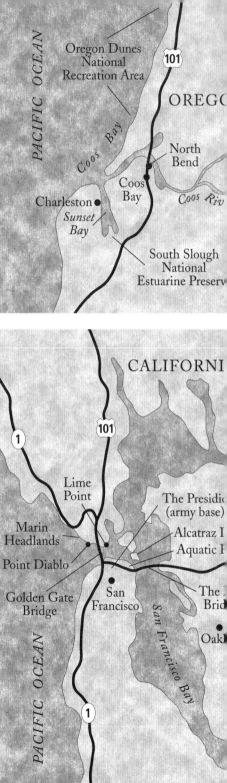

writing a book on sea kayaking. She and her husband, Biges Graves, built kayaks over twenty years ago to paddle Baja California—long before the roads made the access easy.

The museum's curator, Virginia walks me through South Bend's one-room storefront museum. Glass cases of arrowheads and old tools fill the room. On the wall, aged nameboards of lumber schooners hang alongside yellowed photographs of waterfront cedar mills streaking the sky with steam and smoke. The museum's displays tell of a pioneer struggle and a turn-of-the-century heyday when Willapa Bay and Pacific County were a bustling region. Salmon was in abundance, and millions of the bay's oysters were shipped to restaurants in San Francisco.

But it was timber that brought the boosters and entrepreneurs. Boomtowns rose as the timber was felled: South Bend, claimed by a 1904 Pacific County public relations advertisement to be the "Baltimore of the West," was a burgeoning town of three thousand one hundred people—including five lawyers. Today, the town is the county seat and looks much the same as it did in the pictures, without the smoke and steam, and although the current number of lawyers stands at nine, the population is halved. The area is a backwater now, quiet and green. Fast-growing alders and the strength of the tide are subtly reclaiming the land once dominated by the lives of humans.

At South Bend, Coast Highway 101 meets Willapa Bay. The bay is large—122 square miles of tidal estuary, twenty-five miles long, six miles wide. At high tide it is a broad sweep of calm sea, but with the ebb the tidewater drains, leaving miles of rich, pungent mud.

My first encounter with the Willapa tideflats years ago was a tragedy narrowly averted. For some unremembered photographic reason, I walked out on a tideflat, making good progress until I stopped to frame my picture. Some twenty feet from shore, I became stuck.

· THE HIDDEN COAST ·

Attempting to free one foot only caused the other to settle deeper. Sinking slowly above my boot tops, I first worried about my camera, then I began to wonder whether I was ever going to reach solid ground. Dignity was quickly giving way to self-preservation. I realized that the only way I was going to extricate myself, boots or no boots, would be to take the weight off my feet. I leaned forward to break the suction, canting my body farther and farther until I lay spread-eagled on the tideflat, my camera straight-armed out in front of me. I slithered to solid ground, coated from head to my still-booted toes with Willapa Bay mud.

What then is the attraction of kayaking Willapa Bay? Just south of town the highway crosses a series of rivers, one after another, three in less than three miles. Driving over the single-span bridges, you can catch brief, intriguing glimpses of what's upstream. This is the invitation to paddling Willapa Bay—not the open waters, but these winding streams where the tide pushes its way inland.

A legion of British gardeners could not have created a more ordered host of rivers—a total of nine empty into Willapa Bay. They are short as rivers go, some less than five miles long. Their names are a mix of Native and pioneer: Palix, Naselle, Nemah, Niawiakum, North, Beaver, Cedar, Bear, and Bone. Flowing down from the Willapa Hills, their upland streams are typical Northwest sun-dappled creeks, cluttered with fallen timber from past clearcuts and enclosed by the canopy of the returning forests. But where their tributaries merge and the formed rivers meet the tide, the forest of uniform tree-farm second growth unable to tolerate the saltwater is set back from the rivers. Meadows of salt-tolerant grasses and sedges grow on the riverbanks, from a distance looking like well-kept lawns.

This river shall stay nameless—it is one of the nine, each similar, each different, each deserving a visit. This river, like most of its neighbors, is reached by a dirt road that cuts off from the highway and goes a

116

short distance before it stops at a river landing. I arrive too late at night to paddle, so finding a flat, dry spot, I set up my tent and turn in.

In time I adjust to the periodic sound of a passing car, its headlights flickering through the alder and young fir, its road noise penetrating a near-perfect silence. A sound wakes me near dawn—someone or something is monkeying with my kayak on top of my car. I shine my flashlight and the beam strikes an owl, taking advantage of this high point to watch the clearing for prey. It moves like a man working a crick out of his neck, intensely focusing its wide-set eyes and jerking its head in sudden side-to-side movements. I watch until I am wide awake and ready to move. The owl flies as I leave the tent for the kayak.

The best possible launching spot is across roughly twenty feet of mud. But the ooze is firm enough to skate across and I push my kayak ahead of me. At the water's edge, I settle in and shove off the bank, quietly paddling upstream.

Away from the landing the banks grow steep, overhung with the rich growth of late summer grasses. My vision limited, I paddle to one side of the river to see across the flow and above the bank. At every bend there is a break in the vegetation where a smaller slough meets the river. As the bank folds back, I sight along the openings to the treeline, looking for the signs of pioneer homesteads. Before and during the boom years there were people here, living a river existence—working the oyster beds most likely—depending on the river for fish and the meadows for game. I spot a number of weathered posts, the remains of a dock, and go to investigate.

Getting out of a kayak on a muddy, high bank takes the thought and planning of an engineer. You must spread your weight, keep the boat balanced, and stay off steep banks so slick that a misstep means a sure dunking. I test the mud again and leverage up, one foot on semi-solid ground, the other on the centerline of my boat. Using my paddle for a crutch, I bring my weight on shore, mercifully keeping the water out of both boots.

The meadows are mostly grass and silverweed, a pretty, low-lying plant that is salt tolerant and distinctive for its leaf blades, fir-green above and silvery below. The presence of this plant is a sure sign of tidal inundation, no matter how nice a camping spot this field seems to be. I follow the rotted pier back through the grasses to the wall of the fir forest. Whatever was once here on the high ground inside the forest canopy—a home, a logging operation, a still—now is just mossed-over boards. Around and through the site, elk tracks by the hundreds flow along the protective edge of the trees following the course of the river. I follow their route over a treed spur and stop short of the tree margin to scan the next meadow.

There are two big-antlered bucks and a doe grazing not more than fifty feet away. I freeze and watch. Elk are big animals, with brown bodies and a gold rump patch, more solid and beefy than deer and far larger. One or the other watches across the river while the rest feed. It is unusual to see mature males in the open. They are a favorite of the local hunters, and hunting season is two weeks away. Suddenly I clap my hands, an almost involuntary reaction, and startle them back into the relative protection of the forest—to warn them about us. Feeling a little foolish, I watch them go. I scared them—a well-intentioned action of doubtful value to either of us. Sooner or later these bucks will fill a freezer and feed a family.

By the time I return to my kayak, the tide has reversed its course and I paddle toward the landing, watched no doubt by the puzzled eyes of the elk.

COOS BAY: Patchwork Quilt

The *Prince of Tokyo II* is a chip ship, a thirty-eight-thousand-ton,

667-foot-long cargo vessel designed and built for transporting shredded pulpwood to the paper mills of Japan. Negotiating the river bar entrance to Coos Bay, Oregon, she will spend four days loading her holds with forty thousand short tons of wood chips, the equivalent of thirty-two-hundred log truck loads, before returning to Japan.

Once through the jetty, the ship negotiates the curves of the Coos River. She passes a number of active timber mills: Georgia Pacific, Oregon Chip, Roseburg Forest Products, and Weyerhaeuser—some manufacturing logs to lumber, most just exporting chips for paper production. Ghostly skeletons of deserted mills fill in the remaining shoreline, stilled by a century of fierce competition and the rapid depletion of Oregon's old-growth forests.

Beyond the piles of chips and rotting piers lie the old towns of Coos Bay and North Bend, their post-Victorian buildings showing decades of wear and hard times. The streets lie quiet. Vacant lots mark the remaining signatures of once proud structures. Second-hand stores are filled with books, tools, and old "cork" boots. And along Highway 101, the log trucks rumble toward the piers.

At the part of the river known as the North Bend upper range, the *Prince of Tokyo II* begins to turn with the assistance of tugs to make a port-side-to landing beside a mountain of wood chips. Stevedores take her lines, the hatch load points are matched with the great pierside conveyor belts, and the ship is ready to receive cargo.

Beyond the ship, into the haze of the river valley, lie hills covered with the raw earth of clearcuts and with random stands of second- and third-growth timber. A few remnant old-growth trees, known as relics, punctuate the horizon. The scene is an old Northwest quilt, tired and still beautiful, a patchwork of history, industry, and played-out richness pieced together by the sloughs and tributaries of the Coos River.

The tidewater reaches over twenty-five miles up the Coos, past the confluence of the north fork—the Millicoma River—and the South Fork. Even into its headwaters, this is a working river: the hills are logged, the floodplain is fence-to-fence dairy farms. But the river is its own entity, patiently eroding here and building there. Its banks' vegetation of brambles, alder, and cottonwood overruns old landings that once docked the paddlewheel steamboats.

Put-ins here are as scarce as environmentalists. But the South Fork has a public boat launch at about river mile twenty-two. I pull into the boat launch on an early July morning, to catch the fog lifting and the first glimpse of clear blue sky. It's mid-week and there's no one about. I shove off into a three-knot ebb tide mix of fresh river water and tide. The current carries me along, offering me an excuse to set my paddle down and trail my hands in the cool water. The low hum of a summer's day has not begun, and the sun has yet to crest the coast mountains to warm my back. The sweet, spiraling call of a Swainson's thrush awakens the riverbank, and a tractor starts up on a farm bordered by the age-old presence of great oaks.

My kayak drifts and turns at the gentle mercy of the flow of the Coos, my view panning with the swing of the bow. At times the river straightens, and my view expands downstream to take in barn roofs and fog settled in the ravines. With each turn of the river and swing of my boat, the light on the water changes, the advancing dawn adding color to its silver track.

An American flag droops on its pole over one farm between me and a recently logged hillside. This valley must have been logged about one hundred years ago, for the loggers have returned in recent years to harvest the second growth. My upriver view is dominated by the cut-timber hills, and in time my thoughts are occupied by the controversy—the crisis of the last old-growth trees and the future livelihood of the local people. I am fixated on the term "renewable resources"; it bothers me.

· EMBAYMENTS ·

In the Northwest, the logger has always been a romantic figure, a Paul Bunyan type who anchors much of the region's mystique and is the cultural basis of these forested coastal river valleys. But the romance is ending with the felling of the last tall trees—these two-hundred- to five-hundred-year-old giants are not renewable. In Coos County, an area of 1,692 square miles once covered with marketable forests, only an estimated four thousand acres of old-growth timber remains.

It is unlikely that our children's children will ever see a tree farm of two-hundred-year-old Douglas fir, because the dynamics of the multinational forest product conglomerates, so vulnerable to buyouts, foreign investment, and market uncertainty, indicate a return to "cut-and-run" logging of younger and younger trees. Now, as the third- and fourth-generation loggers of Coos County turn their anger on the environmentalists and nature itself, their local job base is shrinking with the size of the trees and they must sense that they too are not renewable resources. With the last of the forest giants goes Paul Bunyan, the romance, and the culture.

It is with some sadness and understanding that I paddle through the Coos River valley. I too used to be a logger—a choker and a timber cruiser. I can feel the dulling of the land's energy and the stubborn pride among its people. I grab my paddle to shake the train of thought. The sun now graces the river, as I approach the first of the towns and the river broadens into the bay. Mile thirteen reveals a ten-square-mile mudflat stretching off to my right, an estuary of channels to play in on a higher tide. I stay within the markers of Marshfield Channel for over a mile, paddling toward the waterfront of Coos Bay.

Five ships are in the harbor loading forest products. Among them is the *Prince of Tokyo II*, already deeper in the water, three days from sailing. Just beyond the Weyerhaeuser pier, I see three boys skipping rocks along the bay's edge. They are the only people I have seen who are not working on the river. Past North Bend, the current turns beneath the great 5,338-foot-long steel truss and concrete bridge that is the unofficial symbol of Coos Bay.

As I paddle out under the bridge, the sea begins to make its presence known. From the pilings of the ghost mills fleets of cormorants take wing, and a pelican lumbers by unperturbed by my passing. A northwest wind blows in from the ocean, slowing my progress. It is this wind that steals sand from the long beach that separates Coos Bay from the Pacific Ocean to create the Oregon Dunes, a forty-mile expanse of steep, blond, sand ridges and remnant forests ending at the northern shore of Coos Bay.

Two miles from the sea, the river makes a final bend past the fishing port of Charleston and the entrance to South Slough National Estuarine Preserve—the nation's first estuarine sanctuary. Two half-mile jetties—riprap arms of rock and rubble—are Coos Bay's last link with land. Still paddling the tail of the ebb, I pull on drawstrings, tighten Velcro, and check my spray skirt closure in anticipation of some standing waves. Arriving at the end of the north jetty, I can just hear the whistle of the sea buoy almost two miles out. It is then that I notice the fog, the first few low wisps swimming by, backlit by the golden afternoon sun. If I go any farther I may be swallowed up, isolated by fog. I turn with the roll of the swell back to Charleston, and the ten-dollar cab ride to my car.

SAN FRANCISCO: Kayaking to Baghdad

The closest I have ever come to having the wind rip a paddle out of my hands was underneath the north tower of the Golden Gate Bridge. It was my first time paddling San Francisco Bay, and like millions of seafarers before me, I wanted to experience the sensation of arriving beneath the Golden Gate. Fresh from the little cove in the lee of five-hundred-foot-high Lime Point, I was solo, life-jacketed, and wide awake. I was making good speed, intending to paddle out against the tide beneath the span, then cross to mid-channel before turning to ride the current back into my favorite city.

But not more than one hundred feet off the point, I got into trouble. The tide was swirling in from the Pacific, creating rips as it surged around the base of the bridge's north pylon. Whirlpools and eddylines ahead had captured all my attention, when a blast of wind descending from the Marin County hills struck me on my right side, caught my paddle blade, and blew me over.

My right hand lost its grip, the shaft pivoting around, twisting my left hand to its full range as I struggled to stay upright. I knew enough to let the paddle go with the wind—just so long as my left hand stayed with it. Once the wind no longer had a surface to oppose, I returned to an upright if hunkered down position.

I had nearly capsized. It would have been sheer luck if I'd been able to execute a successful Eskimo roll—a technique of using body motion and a sweep of the paddle to turn right-side up. But if I had failed, I would have had to exit the boat. Swimming in sixty-degree water and the turbulence of the tide, it would have been difficult to rig a self-rescue system before hypothermia began to take hold. This had been a close call. Between gusts, I got a full grip on the paddle and myself, and backed away from the eddyline to the protection of the point. Once my heartbeat had simmered down, I paddled forward to continue my journey.

Now I find myself, older and possibly wiser, once again paddling from the cove at Lime Point, bound for San Francisco and a breakfast caffe latte. Though the tide is flooding, the rips are fun, and the wind this time is only light air in the predawn morning. It is October, a fresh autumn day in the making, but I am hoping for sunshine. With repeated glances past the San Francisco skyline, I will the clouds over Oakland to part in a picturesque sunrise. The weather gods give me just a piece of the sun, and it rises through a baywide layer of clouds. I photograph what I can, the city backlit in the morning haze that reflects on an undulating sea.

Joining the fishermen speeding out through the Gate, I move quickly, staying close to the Marin shore, taking advantage of back eddies and working the coves toward Point Diablo. An outbound tanker, the *Coast Range*, passes beneath the 225-foot-high span. I follow her progress as she returns to sea, the thumping vibration of her huge propeller resonant through the hull of my boat. Another ship is inbound on the south side of the main vessel traffic lane. The Coast Guard reports roughly eight hundred arrivals and departures of ships of over twenty thousand tons through the Gate in any given month— more than twenty-five ships like the *Coast Range* per day.

I literally look both ways before I begin to cross the channel. These ships cannot maneuver in the narrow, 4,228-foot-wide pass, and their speed is a distance-closing twenty- to twenty-five miles an hour. I turn and paddle toward mid-channel, soaring over the wake of the passing ships. As I near the bridge, the sound of a weekday rush hour is over-shadowed by the neck-craning view of this remarkable symbol of San Francisco, its graceful orange cables strung from 740-foot-high twin towers. I notice a jogger, a tiny silhouette near mid-span, and surprisingly the person waves at me. I break into a grin and wave back.

San Francisco is a city everyone loves. Its nicknames bespeak a special fondness: poet George Sterling has called it "the cool grey city of love," Robert Louis Stevenson "the City of Gold," and William Saroyan "the wild-eyed, all-fired and hard-boiled, tenderhearted white-haired boy of the American family of cities." From the waterfront come "Frisco," "the Pearl of the Orient," "the Golden Gateway," and the

"Queen City of the Pacific." President Calvin Coolidge called it the "Athens of the West," and for obvious if irreverent reasons, some call it "Shakey Town." But it was Herb Caen, the longtime columnist of the *San Francisco Chronicle*, who captured the elusive, quirky quality of this city: he called it "Baghdad by the Bay."

No other American city strikes the newcomer with such promise or such heart. As I pass along the seawall below the Presidio—the old fort, once Spanish and now a U.S. military museum piece—the distant city skyline joins with the rooflines of Pacific Heights in an intricate and elegant jumble of architecture. The late-nineteenth-century and post-1906-earthquake Victorian houses are wall to pastel wall. They fill and lighten the hillsides, enticing would-be residents with their distinctive, colorful facades. Even the street names embellish the aura of the city: Java, Balboa, Cannery, Clipper, and Embarcadero.

Along the seawall, fishermen cast toward me. Behind them looms the great dome of the Palace of Fine Arts, the only remaining building of the Panama Pacific International Exposition of 1915. From my seagoing vantage point, I can imagine that era of simpler problems, tamer war engines, and far fewer people. I follow the waterfront of the city now given over to historic ships and marinas, and duck into Aquatic Park. I steer clear of goggled, capped swimmers lapping the expanse of the manmade boat basin and paddle for shore. Grounding on the sand, I make not a stir among the habitués of this waterfront park. Dragging my kayak higher, I cap it with the coaming cover, and sure of its safety I go in search of a latte, a croissant, and the memory of Herb Caen among the populace.

PADDLE
TO THE SEA

The Columbia River

Hanford Reach to McNary Dam

The rocks slide beneath my keel in water so clear I feel suspended between river and sky. I set my paddle down and drift, running with the current of the Columbia River, letting it dictate my course. All around me water is moving westward. The river's low background noise, which rumbles like distant thunder, is overlain by the suck of whirlpools and the tear of colliding eddies. The sound reverberates against basalt bluffs and sagebrush hills forming the muted words—energy, time, permanence: it is the voice of the Columbia running free, the natural expression of what may be America's most compromised river.

This noble river is no longer the Columbia of Lewis and Clark's day, when the rapids ran on for miles, the whole drainage of over a quarter-million square miles exploding through channels less than fifty yards wide. Today it is still one of the most powerful of our nation's largest rivers, falling farther than any other (2,650 vertical feet) in its journey to the Pacific, but its rapids lie drowned behind eleven major dams in a string of reservoirs about a thousand miles long. Only this

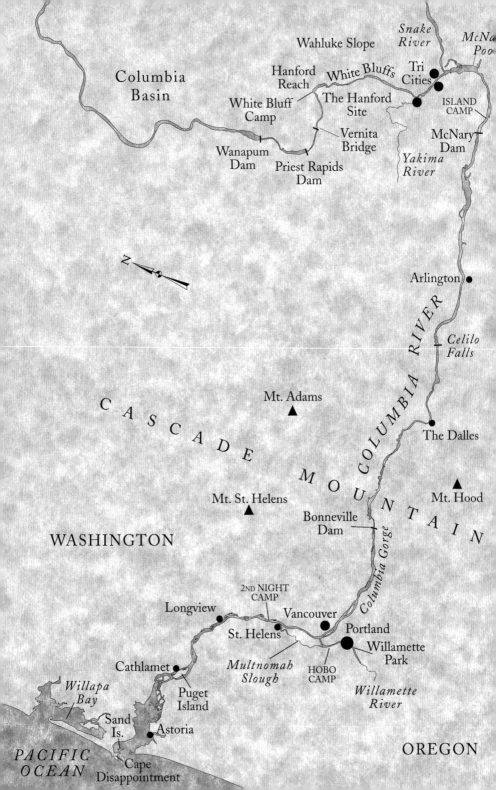

51-mile stretch in the middle of Eastern Washington and the final 145-mile portion of the "tidewater" Columbia remain free flowing. I want to paddle these remnants of what Lewis and Clark and the Corps of Discovery found in 1805—what William Clark called "this great river"—to listen to the language of the Columbia as it is today and, maybe, sense the original Columbia, the one that still has a current, a pulse, a natural history, and possibly a lesson in the boils and backwaters of what lies ahead.

> *As the portage of our canoes over this high rock would be impossible with our Strength . . . I thought by good steering we could pass down safe, accordingly I determined to pass through this place not withstanding the horred appearance of this agitated gut swelling and boiling & whorling in every direction which from the top of the rock did not appear as bad as when I was in it. However we passed safe to the astonishment of the Indians.*
> —William Clark, at Celilo Falls, October 24, 1805

The Columbia River comes to life when it passes through the turbines of the Priest Rapids Dam. Below the tailrace it quickly composes itself as a free-ranging river, shouldering against Umtanum Ridge and moving into more open country. From this point down to the slack water of the McNary Pool, the river is known as the Hanford Reach. Ahead of me stretches Vernita Bridge. I line up between its bastions and paddle through with the current, continuing to work toward the far bank. I relax a little, mindful of the sun setting over my shoulder. The heat of the land is replaced by a river's musty coolness. Clouds too young to be thunderheads dapple the light across an arid landscape of distant blond hills. On either bank, a thin line of black cottonwood, juniper, and white mulberry trees has established itself with the controlled river levels. The trees harbor a sampling of wildlife that seem to play hide-and-seek with me as I pass: legs and torsos of foraging white-tailed deer, the intermittent sight of a male marsh hawk, a collection of standing herons. Then, beyond the tree-line, the shape of an atomic reactor slides into view, one of eight deactivated nuclear reactors that line the Hanford Reach with a lethal ease.

I have paddled into what is known simply as the Hanford Site, 560 square miles of sagebrush desert that was quietly appropriated in 1943 by the Army Corps of Engineers from a sparse population of Native Wanapum people, riverside farmers, and upland ranchers. In the name of the war effort, the towns of White Bluffs and Hanford were bulldozed over, and in the next three years three nuclear reactors were built along the banks of the river to fuel the race for the atom bomb; five additional plutonium production reactors were later built between 1949 and 1955. Their sinister presence is the reason that ninety-six percent of this environment has remained "natural." Never heavily farmed or grazed prior to World War II, today the buffer lands surrounding the Department of Energy's central Hanford complex are a fenced-off western landscape of bunch grass, burrowing owls, and prairie falcons—an undisturbed land of natural complexity and simple beauty with an unpredictable future.

Paddling beside these ziggurat-shaped concrete structures, built before containment domes rounded and softened the nuclear image, I am left with the eerily open-ended contradiction that the last free-flowing part of the river wilderness in the Columbia Basin is protected from agribusiness and dam builders by a profound contamination. Downriver loom the White Bluffs, the beginning of a twenty-mile escarpment that turns the Columbia southward toward the Tri-Cities. I must cross over and soon, if I am to reach the small bay beneath the bluffs and my campsite for the night.

· PADDLE TO THE SEA ·

Every decision a kayaker makes on a moving river must be made early. To cross the Columbia I make my own bargain with the current and the width of the crossing, pointing my kayak upstream, across the flow, eyeing my destination on the far shore. If I am still sliding downstream then I have to point higher and work harder. But I had started early enough to have an easy ferry-glide angle. I paddle quickly across the third-of-a-mile-wide river and gain the back eddy of the cove; the White Bluffs rising to meet me glow in the afterlight of sunset.

My campsite (with the permission of the Department of Energy) is a shelf, an old shoreline where the pre-dam Columbia had cut a bench during its more rambunctious days. There is an old fire ring, and above the bank a farmer's windbreak of dying black locust trees planted decades ago. It is windless and warm off the water, and once I have dragged my kayak above the high-water mark and laid out my gear, it is quiet too. Well, sort of quiet. I settle in, listening to the arriving sounds of the nightshift on the Hanford Reach: beavers, bats, coyotes, and owls all gnawing, darting, howling, and grasping about, at times within feet of my campsite.

~~~

The White Bluffs are an early Pleistocene sandstone/siltstone formation of continuous cliffs that jump out of the sage-green Eastern Washington landscape like a dazzling yellow-white grin. As I paddle downstream, they are the stage set of my spring morning education at the Hanford Reach. The cliffs are an inverted suburb some three hundred feet high for an avian community of both rare and routine: Copper-blue cliff swallows are at the river's edge gathering mud in their beaks for their gourd-like nests in the overhangs. Rock doves (pigeons to any urban dweller) flying in pairs glide across the cliffs warily eyeing, one would assume, the peregrine falcons, also in pairs, that work out over the river and then arc back to gain the thermals off the cliffs, often communicating with an anxious high-pitched call that can signify an aerie nearby. High above the rim are the black silhouettes of the ubiquitous ravens, most likely scouting the game trails that parallel the river's course. Staying close to the cliff, I paddle directly beneath a lone mulberry miraculously anchored to the base of the bluffs. Among its branches I stare into the large yellow-black eyes of a short-eared owl. I am so close she relies on stillness rather than flight to save herself. To give this natural community some peace (there are some 184 species of birds, 39 mammals, 9 reptiles, and 4 amphibians that call the Reach home), I ferry across to the other side.

The western shore is the "hot" side of the river, a flat basalt plain between the Columbia and the western rise of Rattlesnake Ridge. Here, along with the nuclear reactors that produced plutonium for World War II, are the old reprocessing "canyons," the factories that reprocessed irradiated nuclear fuel, the waste tanks, and landfills that are now undergoing a slow cleanup attempt. For unfortunately, in the rush to win the war, radioactive waste was routinely cached in these tanks and earthen pits which are now leaking into the groundwater and seeping toward the Columbia. I am paddling toward a shoreline that is constantly monitored for contamination; it lies in what may be the largest public works effort in the history of the U.S. government, whose purpose is just to return the area to safe and sane sagebrush.

Out of the main current along the western shore, I paddle through a set of gravel shallows that are the most precious natural treasure of the Reach. As the 1992 Draft Environmental Impact Statement for the Hanford Reach stated: "The Hanford Reach is the only stretch of the Columbia River supporting healthy populations of native fish that evolved under free-flowing aquatic conditions." Sixty percent of the Columbia River fall Chinook salmon spawn in the riffles of the

· PADDLE TO THE SEA ·

Hanford Reach from October to early November. Lewis and Clark witnessed this magnificent salmon run when they scouted the Reach in October 1805. The Corps of Discovery was amazed at the millions of fish spawning and dying along the Columbia's banks. As I drift over the spawning beds of the Hanford Reach, I can see where the gravel was shoved aside last fall by the fins and flanks of the exhausted fish that had ascended the fish ladders of four major dams. Gravel depression overlapping depression reminds me of the abundance that the explorers witnessed, and I reflect on the fact that today, this wild salmon bed is the only healthy one on the entire river.

The multitudes of this fish are almost inconceivable. The water is so clear that they can readily be seen at the depth of 15 or 20 feet; but at this season they float in such quantities down the stream, and are drifted ashore, that the Indians have only to collect, split, and dry them on the scaffolds.
—William Clark, at the confluence of the Yakima and the Columbia Rivers, near the current town of Richland, Washington, October 17, 1805

The river that Lewis and Clark experienced returned an estimated ten to fifteen million salmon annually. Today the river sustains less than one-tenth of that, which alarms a wave of Native peoples, scientists, federal and state agencies—people concerned that these magnificent fish might fail by our hand. It is a battle on many fronts to save the salmon: to prevent the tiny fingerlings or smolts from being ground up in the dams' turbines, to redirect the river's waters away from the marginally beneficial farms, to ensure that the instream flow is cold enough, fast enough, and simply water enough to get the youngsters to the Pacific and to return them as adults to their ancestral streams. Commercial,

Native, and sport fishers need to find common ground and common sense. We need to accept that the hatchery system is not a solution. The battle for the salmon means protecting the river from radioactive waste and it means taking down or successfully bypassing dams.

It is the dams that prevent a resurgence of the Columbia River salmon. In the 1930s, the Army Corps of Engineers chose not to build a salmon bypass or fish ladder on the Bonneville dam. Only a last-minute effort by local Natives, fishers, and concerned citizens forced the Corps to build a fish ladder, thus preventing the permanent loss of eighty-five percent of the Columbia's salmon spawning habitat. (The Corps then failed to design a bypass for Grand Coulee dam, permanently closing more than one-third of the Columbia's drainage to spawning salmon) As recently as 1971, the Corps lobbied to dredge the Hanford Reach for barge traffic. Not surprisingly, with the arrival of fall each year, one by one the salmon tributaries have gone quiet.

But it is difficult to reverse the attitudes and excesses of sixty years. The four thousand farms dependent on the Columbia Basin Irrigation Project use more water than the California State Water Project, which serves over twenty-one million people. Weighed against the possible curtailment of their subsidy, they do not see the value of saving salmon, nor do they see the value of saving what remains of the wilderness habitat of Eastern Washington.

For the past thirty years, there has been a continual effort by agribusiness to convince the Department of Energy that the buffer lands surrounding the Hanford Reach should be turned over to farming. In addition to the 11,000 square miles of farmland already irrigated in the Columbia Basin Project, they want to add the 140-square-mile Wahluke Slope. Currently, the habitat that includes the White Bluffs is being studied by The Nature Conservancy's biologists and others coordinated by the Department of Energy. The field researchers are finding new plants and new insects; in all, ninety new-to-science species are expected to be found in this area and the remaining Hanford Site buffer. The fact that we don't know what natural richness exists there seems reason enough to leave it alone, for the consequences of disregarding the nature of the Wahluke Slope are clear, as I paddle beyond the Wahluke habitat: irrigated farm runoff seeping into the watertable has destabilized the bluff, parts of which have slumped into the river, smothering the riverbed downstream and any salmon eggs that may be buried there.

∿∿

The landslide, a sight of pump houses, a few orchards rimmed by poplars, and a modest trophy house or two—I am paddling out of a reverie. The wilderness of the Hanford Reach, of the White Bluffs, of Lewis and Clark ends in the outskirts of the Tri-Cities: Richland, Pasco, and Kennewick—towns joined at the confluence of the Columbia, the Yakima, and Snake Rivers. Somehow the river has become smaller even as it broadens with the combined flows. It feels less powerful reflected in the picture windows of this riverine suburb. Nature now appears homeless between manicured lawns and park strips. I paddle past the point where the Corps of Discovery first saw the Columbia. There is a state park there named after Sacajawea, the Shoshone woman who acted as interpreter on the journey. The spot of grass and cottonwoods is surrounded by cement plants, grain terminals, tug and barge offloading piers, petroleum depots, and ag-chemical storage facilities. Paddling beneath the bridges of the Tri-Cities, I have entered a different land on an entirely different river.

We were visited this morning by several canoes of Indians. . . . We informed them, as we have done all the other Indian nations, of our friendship for them, and our desire to promote peace among all our

red children in this country. . . . Having completed the purpose
of our stay, we now began to lay in our stores. Fish being out of
season, we purchased forty dogs, for which we gave small articles,
such as bells, thimbles, knitting needles, brass wire, and a few beads,
the exchange of which they all seemed perfectly satisfied.

    —William Clark, at the confluence of the Columbia
    and Snake Rivers, October 18, 1805

The Columbia in 1805 was a trade route, a food source, a gathering
place. Today it is no different except for the scale and value placed
upon the river. The Native Yakama or Nez Perce—or for that matter
the Corps of Discovery—could not have imagined anything man-made
subduing the Columbia. Both shores of the Columbia now rumble with
trains and highways. A navigable waterway, a taxpayer-purchased series
of locks, not for salmon but for grain and oil barges to bypass the great
dams, extends up the Columbia and its main tributary, the Snake River,
all the way into Idaho. Today it is a road, a sewer, a faucet, a light bulb,
a plaything. There is little awe or respect for the river itself. There are
no rapids, and as I paddle west toward Wallula Gap I realize there is
no current—the river is slowing, the Hanford Reach has met the
McNary Pool.

    Paddling across these eerily still waters, a placid lake, or a pool as
the power industry calls the potential energy held in the reservoir above
the McNary dam, I look at the river charts to see the submarine topography the dam inundated. With a little imagination I can see the rapids
that once confronted Lewis and Clark, who ran them in their dugout
canoes. Beneath my boat was a river often split by basalt islands and
obstructions, there were narrow channels, back-eddy pools, and a few
placid reaches, but above all, falls and rapids on a scale greater than any
river I have run, Grand Canyon of the Colorado included. I look away

from the chart across this mile-wide lake with a feeling not unlike grief, longing to see the river as it once was.

I enter Wallula Gap and take refuge in the rising canyon around me. To my right and left, grand basalt terraces, a rich brown with chartreuse lichen in ordered eight-sided ranks, march up to the sky. I can hear canyon wrens with their descending, curling call, and nothing else save the rush of Interstate 84 on the Oregon side. I move to the quieter Washington shore to compensate, paddling over the site of the Corps of Discovery's camp on the night of October 18, 1805. No beaches here, just a broken rock bed called riprap for a rail line that skirts the terraces and bridges the clefts cut by now-dry falls.

Five miles into Wallula Canyon the wind arrives. It is suddenly blowing upriver about ten knots, then fifteen. I hug the shore and paddle on, expecting this, wondering how I can have been so lucky to have gotten this far without wind in the first place. I paddle for miles against winds to twenty knots, waves to two feet, through a wind-flagged, sun-baked country. I become so inured to the steady force and dulling nature of the wind that, head lowered and forearms pumping, I practically run into the one and only good campsite I would encounter on the McNary Pool—the long, thin island of basalt twenty to thirty feet from the Washington side rears up in front of my bow like a ship. A small beach on the inside of the island affords a short climb to a flat, ungrazed wildflower meadow complete with a basalt topknot that provides a windbreak for my tent and kitchen. It begins to rain, I put up the tent, throw in what I want to keep dry, and rig a tarp—so the rain can stop—which it does. It is 9:30 by the time dinner is cooked, Joel fed, Patrick O'Brian opened, and maybe two pages read before I fall asleep.

The next day the wind has increased to twenty-five knots steady. I curl back into my bag and open my book for a rest day. But by mid afternoon I am restless. The wind still twenty-five knots with an endless set of massive whitecaps rolling upriver, I decide to climb the basalt walls of the canyon opposite my island. Moving up a precarious talus of broken basalt, I find a game trail that leads me along a terrace and to a level approach to the rim. I enjoy walking through the steep grassland slopes, keeping an eye out for arrowheads (I have never found one yet), moving steadily toward the top of what must be an eight-hundred-foot vertical rise. What did I expect at the top? A sagebrush landscape? No, it is agribusiness, with laborers plowing right to the rim, raw earth stretching flat across the Columbia Plateau as far as I can see. I retreat quickly back to my island refuge, my book, and my camp stove, numb to our stunning pioneer thoroughness. The wind still howls over my basalt backstop.

By 9:00 the next morning I am under way, facing a gentler ten-knot wind, again staying to the Washington side, working every stroke. I have thirteen miles to go and it takes four-plus hours. As I approach the thin concrete rim which is all that is visible of the McNary Dam, 293 miles from the mouth of the Columbia, I am ready to get off the river. Alienated, yes. Lake Umatilla below the dam is just another McNary pool. I aim for the town side, Umatilla, Oregon, to take out. Siting what looks to be a park, I land on an empty beach amidst proper shade trees, perfect grass with little sprinklers spigotting about, and a sign that says McNary Park, the Army Corps of Engineers. It is as if I have been netted by the Corps, an environmental fish lying on the beach, flopping about in frustration, trying make sense of what we have done to this river and to ourselves.

Portland to the Pacific

The country is low, rich and thickly wooded on each side of the river.
The islands have less timber, but are furnished with a number of

ponds near which are vast quantities of fowls, such as swans, geese, brants, cranes, storks, white gulls, cormorants, and plovers. The river is wide and contains a great number of sea-otters (Enhydris marina).

—William Clark, below the confluence of Sandy River, in today's eastern suburbs of Portland, Oregon, November 3, 1805

I call it the tidewater Columbia because of its meandering ways, its mile-wide breadth, its brackish give and take with the sea. Once the Columbia River passes through the Cascade Mountains it leaves behind the shrub-steppe sun, the basalt canyons, the reservoirs, and the dams for a world of fog and rain, forested hills, sea gulls, and weathered wharfs. It is a mature river now, moving through a green open valley and forming long comma-shaped river islands with its braided channels and resurgent tides. And it is a river with a settler's history of clapboard towns that have matured into cities. It is for this sense of history that I choose Portland to resume paddling the free-flowing Columbia. I want to put in not below the last dam but in the heart of this city on the Willamette River, to see the heritage of its backwaters from a small boat and to experience Portland's relationship with the river that gives the city its link with the sea. My choice could not have been better.

Willamette Park is the perfect put-in in perfect mayhem. It is a Saturday afternoon with blue skies, ninety-four degrees, Portland's four-cycle nautical set is in liquid ecstasy: jet skis in a blue haze are jumping wakes of Ski Nautiques moving at freeway speeds and narrowly missing deep-water cigarette boats incongruously thundering about on a river about a quarter of a mile wide. The members of a sailing class, gaff-rigged prams with white sails rocking, are clustered together in midstream like circled wagons, while now and then a simple aluminum skiff skitters for safety at a steady seven knots, the occupants well-resigned to the constant wakes rebounding off a ragged shore. At the boat launch, center stage of this maritime opera, I pack my kayak quickly amid the exuberance and exhaust, and thread my way out on the Willamette River, pointing downstream through the flash of white fiberglass and day-glow pink bikinis toward the Rose City and the Pacific.

Paddling into the downtown energy I realize I am in the midst of more than just a fine Saturday afternoon. The city's annual bash, the Rose Festival, is in full swing. Nosing along past the visiting U.S. Navy frigates and destroyers, I greet the sailors leaning against the rails. Beyond them an itinerant carnival gyrates along the seawall against a backdrop of new high-rises and house-dotted hills. There are crowds of people strolling, flirting, enjoying a riverfront of new parks, sculpture, restaurants, and running paths. Portland is booming, changing. New housing developments are infilled between old flour mills and derelict piers. Some of the old structures are being turned into new Internet and computer software startup offices, and the river-dependent industries that made this city, the shipyards, canneries and log dumps, timber mills and grain terminals, for the most part have either moved downriver or just plain moldered away, their rotting pilings waving in the wake of reinvented paddlewheel steamboats and dinner cruise yachts.

By the eighth river mile, well below the waterfront festival, I paddle into Portland's port facilities, its container piers and chemical and petroleum companies silhouetted against an evening sky. This is a larger, more complex version of the earlier river industries, less river-dependent in a global economy yet potentially more environmentally damaging. A six-thousand-horsepower tug of the type that replaced the Columbia River steamboats passes me on the port side headed for her company pier. A shipyard is highlighted in the flash and shadow of arc welders, its drydocks cradling two Keystone tankers, one so large it dwarfs a worker painting white depth numbers fifty-five feet down her deep red hull.

Amid this shoreline now dominated by concrete and chain-link, I begin to scout for a camp. A small marina tucked behind the shipyard looks promising, but the access is secured. I scout and reject a few development sites as they are too raw or inaccessible. The first beach of any size appears to have once been a petroleum transshipment facility, but it is posted like a crime scene by the EPA: NO FISHING HAZARDOUS WASTE SITE ENVIRONMENTAL PROTECTION AGENCY. Then I spy a copse of alders on the opposite bank. In the growing dusk I can just make out the promise of a beach as I ferry-glide over to a sandy shore, a jumble of drift logs, two white-walled tires with some miles on them, and one heron that flies reluctantly at my approach. I check the terrain for a hobo's camp, and finding none, I nose ashore.

My tiny riverside refuge is a welcome home for the night. I throw up my tent and light the stove. With darkness falling, I chop, cut, cook, eat, clean, listen, and watch the river, a contented contemporary Huck Finn well aware of what the river has provided. Underlying the adventure of my day is a growing feeling of hope in the change on the Willamette. Portland's focus is returning to the river with the seeds of a broader understanding: playing on the water as well as working on it, living beside the river and becoming aware of its problems. The city is cleaning up the Willamette even if it takes the courts to force action. I can sense a sea change, a collective awareness of our responsibility for the health and diversity of all the rivers we live beside.

~~~

It is the beginning of a warm and windless summer day. My refuge camp one highway and one rail bridge behind me, I am paddling near midstream, steeling for the job of kayaking eight to ten hours on the water. Wisely or not, I have only three full days for the 103 miles remaining to the mouth of the Columbia. But aided by a river current of up to three miles an hour, and if the west winds do not blow, I know I can do it. I return my chart to its deck case and make a decision. Ahead of me the Willamette branches, the greater flow meeting the Columbia three miles distant, the lesser breaking west into Multnomah Channel, a slower tree-lined side slough one- to two-hundred yards wide and twenty-one miles long. I choose the Twain-like simplicity of the slough, which bustles with the avuncular river-rat energies that sloughs tend to attract: strings of houseboats in various stages of improvement and/or disintegration, a poor man's marina (bilge pumps a-running), and other backwater dreams are tied to the Portland side or to the right along the levees protecting the dairy farms of Sauvie Island. In a few miles even these river uses dwindle into a sylvan riverscape—something approaching wilderness interrupted by the occasional baying of cows.

After eight hours of paddling I am nearing the confluence of the slough and the Columbia. It comes suddenly. Kayaking around a bend and seeing into the distance, I pass out of a hallway of trees to an expanse of water that rolls back to an immense sky. It is as if I have burst onto a stage filled with vigorous current, cottonwood backdrops, and ocean-going ships. The river seems to dwarf the clear-cut hills on the Washington bank and the treed lowlands of the Oregon side. Nature crowds the shore, returning, reclaiming, overgrowing 150 years of pioneer effort. And the Columbia, a deep afternoon blue, takes my kayak and hastens me west.

Riding the big water, chart in hand, I look downstream. I am below Sauvie Island now, passing the small, comfortable Oregon town of St. Helens, where everyone seems to be at the river's edge enjoying the cool of the evening. A couple sits back-to-back on the marina dock, kids on the shore skip stones, a group of teenagers stands immobile like cormorants on a seawall, boaters laze on their afterdecks, hibachis smoking. The jet skis and cigarette boats are gone. Time is flirting with the sultriness of summer, caught up in the quiet commotion of the river's movement.

Suddenly from a shore of waterfront houses a man rushes out on his deck and shouts across the water to me; I catch the word "Astoria?"

"Yes, Astoria bound," I yell, anchoring my trip for him to the last town before the mouth of the Columbia and the open ocean. He waves enthusiastically and we share an odd, fine satisfaction that I am headed for the last port, the last landfall, the last reach of the Columbia, and the Pacific, so long as I keep paddling. At the next marina I stop to buy a pack of Lifesavers and to refill my water jugs to celebrate rejoining the great river. I shove into the current hoping to make at least another five miles on the day.

Below Portland, the Columbia is braided with islands that from my on-river vantage point appear to be a solid line of trees. But then a break appears marking the upstream end of an island. A spit leads upstream, with first willows then alder and cottonwood—a perfect campsite. I paddle right to compensate for the river current and gain the riverside of the island. I pick a spot high enough and open enough to come ashore. Once my boat is tied above the debris line, I stretch— unbend is more accurate—and begin to set camp, serenaded with a robin's evening song and warmed by the last of the sun setting through the trees.

It isn't until I align my tent into the wind that I realize the wind is blowing up the valley, fresh and clear from the sea. Through the pasta boiling and the vegetables sautéing, I reflect on my being seventy-six miles from the Columbia Bar. This wind might be the same wind that stopped me at Umatilla, the same wind that has made the Columbia Gorge the windsurfing capital of the world. Now it is beginning to blow through the willows of what I call Second Night Island, putting an edge on what has been a perfect paddling day.

The next morning is clear, cool and, to my surprise, windless. I hurry into my boat and curl into the spring-green world of a backside slough. This is a river forest of tenuous majesty. The current teases my kayak into lesser channels, and the sloughs take me where the trees pattern the sky. I startle a bittern who labors up into the heavy air and through the canopy. In the returning stillness comes the sound of earth tumbling into the river, erosion a constant of these river islands. Fallen cottonwood sweepers lie across the water, vibrating in the current, while freshly silted side channels grow thickets to replace them in an ever-evolving island wilderness molded and bent by the muscle of the river.

The natural character of the lower Columbia surprises me. Not just the islands in mid-stream but both the Oregon and Washington shores are sparsely populated. Gone are the more than eighty salmon canneries that lined the river of 1866. Gone too are the hundreds of independent logging operations and lumber mills that polluted every town from Portland to the sea with wood smoke. Now their legacy is a few massive operations at St. Helens, Longview, and Astoria. As I paddle by a measured string of pilings that once anchored the many mill-bound log booms, I can only imagine the rambunctious past of sailing scows and steamboats, log flues, salmon traps, gillnetters, and iron chinks. It was a romantic yet heedless sort of progress that fished, cut, and eventually damned this river to exhaustion. Oddly, what remains after the settlements and camps disappeared is this quiet, sterile, yet beautiful river world sculpted by the current and power of the Columbia.

As I approach the town of Kalama, a foothill spur of the Cascades hardens both the Oregon and Washington sides, narrowing and speeding up the river. I move away from the morning fog of the Oregon shore

◄◄ *Sunset, mist, black rocks—dinner goes cold with the fleeting moments of a summer evening sky.*

▲ *Surf kayakers ride the inner break—waves to eight feet—at La Push, Washington.*

◄ *The nine rivers of Willapa Bay wind to quiet ends among the boughs of cedar and the tracks of elk crossing muddy sloughs.* ◄▼ *On my first paddle of San Francisco Bay, I head beneath the Golden Gate Bridge, into the wind and a near knockdown.* ► *A mountain of wood chips dwarfs a "chip ship" at the Oregon port of North Bend.* ▼ *Sunrise on the Coos River.*

◄◄ *Coyote tracks follow the rim of the White Bluffs above Hanford Reach on the Columbia River.*
◄ *Architecture of World War II, the Hanford Site B reactor decays in the afternoon sun.*
▼ *An Upland larkspur, one of the many wildflower species of Umtanum Ridge.* ▼▼ *Paddling the working Columbia past a pulp mill at St. Helens, Oregon.*

151

◄ Each arch is a different experience, depending on the tide height, sea swell, and hidden reefs. Will Cooper negotiates a small free-standing arch with a tricky set of entry reefs on the north side of Cape Meares. ▲ Steller's sea lions and suburbia meet along the Oregon coast, at Three Arch Rocks, Oceanside, Oregon. ▼ Sun strikes the mouth of the Mattole River and sand blows against my legs. Even at dawn the wind sculpts the Lost Coast. ►► Anacapa's north coast has caves of Hollywood dimensions—so big, all of us fit.

◄◄ *The other-worldly form of a* pitaya dulce *cactus frames the desert coastline of Baja California and the Sea of Cortez in December morning light.* ▲ *The mystical El Coyoté Bay, Bahía de Concepción, wakes to "Tap" Tappley coaxing an outboard to life.* ◄ *A rooster fish meets the food chain in the form of Charley Fiala.* ▼ *Kayakers scud before the wind at five-plus knots. The peaks of the Sierra de la Giganta mountains pass in the distance.* ► *Silhouetted in the sun, a monumental sea stack, home of an osprey family, overshadows a sea kayaker in San Juanico Cove.*

◄◄ *Sleepy La Manzanilla awakens, and townspeople come to barter and buy the fishermen's catch.* ◄▼ *"The Churches," a set of small sea stacks, challenge kayakers with their narrow channels and sea surges off La Manzanilla.* ◄ *A great white heron perches in the crown of a mangrove tree moments before its shy flight.* ▼ *In mangroves, a ready ear and a quick eye discover hidden life in the shade and foliage.* ►► *The pleasure of a western shore—a warm evening, still air, and the setting sun along the Pacific coast of Mexico.*

toward mid-channel to find the best current through Bybee Ledge Channel and then the Kalama Upper Range. Paddling easily through sunlit waters against a mild upstream breeze, I marvel at the way the Columbia carries me along. The current imparts such a sense of purpose to the river that I am caught up in a feeling not unlike being cared for, escorted, as if my mom were taking me to school. I realize the river has become something more to me than a geographic wonder, something more than a vehicle. It is becoming familiar, comfortable, connecting me to its nature as it moves me along. I am beginning to know the river the way you know a friend, to learn from it as if from a teacher. But trusting it is another issue altogether.

I make fifteen nautical miles before 9:00 the next morning. By lunch, twenty-nine, but by two in the afternoon the five-knot breeze that has cooled me throughout the day has become a twenty- to twenty-five-knot blow, a normal windspeed for the lower Columbia when weather is arriving from the Pacific. I cinch up my spray skirt and clear the chart case from my forward deck, leaving the protection of a lunch island to plow into three-foot seas. Winds are both dumping off the high hills on the Washington side and bending with the path of the river, creating a wind convergence zone and standing waves. I work to the calmer north bank and hug the shore while giant freighters churn heedlessly by.

Rounding what is known as Cape Horn, I meet the direct force of the wind. Paddling becomes a matter of technique and strength where every stroke has to be fast, long, and strong. Squinting into the sun, taking a chill spray, I stay as close to the beach as my keel allows, hiding from the wind in the lift of the land and trying to remember just how far Cathlamet, the next downstream town, is from Cape Horn—three miles, five? The chart is buried and I am not going to lose ground by stopping to retrieve it. My pace reminds me of supplicants making a pilgrimage on their knees, as I creep along eyeing the immediate shore in exquisite detail: volcanic rock, drift log, more rock, spray in the face, cottage, boat shed, dock, riprap. Just above Puget Island, windsurfers skim toward me, acknowledge the ridiculousness of my situation, and tack away at thirty miles an hour. When I begin setting paddling goals of not more than a hundred feet away instead of miles, I know I cannot make Cathlamet. The sun is setting behind a low fog bank as I pass a series of unused road-end fish camps beneath high cliffs. I pick the one with a tiny beach and a flat spot for my tent and settle in for the night, wondering where Lewis and Clark camped—they too found the going tough in these parts.

> We could not for several miles find a place sufficiently flat to suffer us to sleep in a level position; at length, by removing some large stones, we cleared a place fit for our purpose above the reach of the tide, and after a journey of 29 miles slept among the smaller stones under a mountain to our right.
>
> November 7th The morning was rainy and the fog so thick that we could not see across the river, the upper point of an island [Puget Island] between which and the steep hills on the right we proceeded for five miles [passing the present site of Cathlamet]."
>
> —William Clark, one mile below Cape Horn,
> November 6 and 7, 1805

4:30 A.M., gray weather, some wind, hot cereal. The front has moved through in the night, bringing the lower Columbia to its more natural state of evergreen and off-white. I paddle bundled up for the first time in the trip, moving downriver beneath a low, dry cloud cover. My goal is a group of islands at the mouth of the Columbia, forty-four miles downstream, or at least to Astoria, ten miles from the mouth. I am in tidewater now, timing my departure with the first of the ebb, staying with the fastest current, even if it means dodging big ships in mid-channel. Puget Island Reach and Turn, Steamboat Reach, Skamokawa Channel Range, Welch Island Reach, the navigation aids fly by as I begin to hug the steeply sloped Washington side with its small cannery bays and early morning steelhead fishers. Below Jim Crow Point, the river begins to widen, creating a maze of channels, marshes, sand islands, sloughs, and creeks. I can sense the ocean in the change.

> Great joy in camp, we are in view of the Ocian, this great Pacific Octian which we have been so long anxious to see, and the roreing or noise made by the waves breaking on the rockey shores (as I suppose) may be heard distinctly.
>
> —Meriwether Lewis, November 7, 1805

The weather kept the Corps of Discovery to the Washington shore, while I strike across the estuary toward Astoria. Beneath the Golden Gate–like Astoria bridge, a fixture in my vision for the past ten miles, I find a fine beach directly underneath its span and come ashore.

Astoria is strung out along a hilly peninsula looking something like it did in pictures of its 1880s heyday (fifty-five canneries in the delta, fifty-four saloons, 7,200 people then, compared to eight canneries/fish packers, seventeen saloons (and lounges), and 11,200 people today). The houses are old, simple, high-peaked, and well-kept. There are still a few surviving wood-frame hotels and boarding houses beside the river that took in sailors, fishermen, itinerant laborers, prostitutes, and card sharks. The commercial district rebuilt after the fire of 1922 is folksy and vibrant; the hills rise up out of the street grid forestalling today's culture-deadening malls. I walk stiffly into town with time on my hands until the floodtide slacks and reverses. Searching out a restaurant, I order clam chowder, fish and chips, and the salad bar, and I stay until I have a blue sky out the restaurant window. After refilling my water bottles and purchasing the luxury of a half pint of half-and-half, I shove off into a just-turned tide.

As the Columbia approaches the Pacific, the river expands from an average width of three-quarters of a mile to seven miles in the Gray's Bay, Harrington Point Range, twenty-one miles from the sea. At the Astoria bridge it is four miles wide, and then the stream narrows to not more than two miles wide where it meets the ocean between the North Jetty and Clatsop Spit. On a map it looks like a large, benign inlet. But this is the Columbia at spring flood, heavy with silt, joining the pull of what is now an energetic ebb tide. As I paddle my way diagonally toward Sand Island, the last of the river islands and my intended camp, I begin to steer around the increasing number of riffles that mark shallow sandbars. There are groins, upright lines of pilings placed to keep the river in its navigation channel, that create both a barrier and turbulence immediately downstream. It is becoming a challenge to get where I want to go. Pointing higher across the increasing current, I work my way to my destination, the upstream end of Sand Island, and pull my kayak ashore. Only a few minutes later, as the river begins to surge past my beach at a speed I could not have sustained, do I realize that I made the eight-mile crossing from Astoria to Sand Island at exactly the right time. But I am neither the first nor the last to underestimate the forces at play where the Columbia meets the sea. Lewis and Clark, moving down the Washington side, camped within eyesight of my island, only to be battered by repeated storms and high tides.

The wind was still high from the southwest, and drove the waves against the shore with great fury; the rain too fell in torrents, and not

'only drenched us to the skin, but loosened the stones on the hillsides, which then came rolling down upon us. In this comfortless situation we remained all day, wet, cold, with nothing but dried fish to satisfy our hunger; the canoes in one place at the mercy of the waves, the baggage in another, and all the men scattered on floating logs, or sheltering themselves in the crevices of the rocks and hillsides.
—William Clark, Gray's Bay, November 11, 1805

Sand Island is lobster-shaped, claws pointing seaward, roughly a mile square in area, surrounded by seabirds, frequented by river otters, and home to a somewhat compact coyote. Above the high tide line, beyond the first line of thorny shrubs, a jumble of driftlogs and ubiquitous plastic bottles begins a low, rolling, treeless topography of beach grasses and wild flowers. A botanist would love this place, I think, as I walk the upper beach toward a sun-silhouetted groin that supposedly anchors this island. There is a bald eagle on one of its pilings, and beyond the loafing bird the Cape Disappointment light winks white then red. Past this last headland lies the Pacific, its swells crashing hard against the Oregon side two miles distant. Tomorrow my plan is to wait for near slack ebb and then paddle out this channel over the Columbia Bar and into the Pacific. But as I had learned this afternoon, the conditions have to be right.

The following morning I awake early and follow fresh coyote tracks out toward the jetty again. It is cool, perhaps fifty-one degrees and overcast, the clouds just clearing the lighthouse roof one mile seaward. The wind is light air from the sea. The conditions are good. I return to camp, start coffee, and rummage for the glorious half-and-half, all the while watching the currents off Sand Island sort themselves out.

The time to go actually catches me by surprise. One moment the current is outgoing and the next it is slack, at least off my camp. I study the main flow of the Columbia about a third of a mile over, still outgoing about three knots. The slack at the mouth, according to the current tables, is 9:24 A.M. It was 8:50 now. The bar conditions on the radio are good. I finish loading, shove off, and instantly get threatened by the Sand Island groin. There is more current out here than I expect. Clearing the last of the pilings, scooting away from the sound of water urgently fighting through the old barrier, I war over my decision to launch. Too much current? Am I too early? What is the bar like? The forecast is for six- to eight-foot swells, but I wonder what the period or space is between crests as these swells move in from the Pacific along my route; too close together and a lone paddler in a seventeen-foot kayak can have his paddle full. Passing the lighthouse, a Coast Guard helicopter flies over, headed up the Washington coast, which reminds me to check my marine radio. When I come level with the base of the North Jetty on the Washington side, I can see that the swells are not breaking on the bar. It looks okay. I check for ship traffic—there is none, save for a few returning fishing boats and a stationary dredge three miles offshore. With each paddle stroke, the Pacific opens to my view. I check the current by watching the riprap pass on the jetty; still fast. Ahead, the swells are not six to eight feet, more like ten to twelve in close order, the current stacking the waves, shortening the period. And among them a final navigation aid on the Columbia—a buoy designated "QG 7 bell."

I now know the Columbia is playing with me as it has all seafarers who have dared the river bar: two thousand known shipwrecks have occurred more or less in this very spot. Twenty-foot breakers are not unheard of where QG 7 is anchored. As I approach the buoy clanging off my starboard bow, I can see it lean with the current, tailing out to sea. "I think this is about as far as I want to go," I shout to the river, as I pull out the camera to frame the buoy, a gray sea looking absurdly flat in the distance. I turn amid the largest of the swells, stealing a glance back behind me as one these odd-sequenced waves picks up my kayak and drives it forward. On my left the buoy clangs again. I am even with it. Five minutes of workmanlike paddling later, I am still even with it.

After a hundred yards gained in two hundred strong strokes, my mind accepts three things: that I was early for the slack current, that this one spot where Clatsop Spit and the North Jetty pinches the river is most likely the fastest current in the mouth of the Columbia, and that I am not completely in control of the situation. I need a solution now or I will have to accept the current and head out to sea. I begin marking what progress I am making against the rocks of the North Jetty. "Hard strokes," I shout out loud. And then I see the answer. Unlike on the Oregon side, here on the side of the jetty fronting the river there are no ten- to twelve-foot swells tearing themselves apart along its flank. The current that stacks these swells must also be taming them. But that does not wholly explain the calm water against the mile-long jetty wall. There must be a back eddy. I angle left to meet the jetty and begin to make headway. And then it is obvious—I am in a fine back eddy taking me right toward the protection of Cape Disappointment.

Beneath the cliffs of the cape there is a beach. It is quiet in outgoing tide conditions, a polite surf, deer grazing on the headland. Tourists from Fort Canby State Park come here to see the Cape Disappointment light flashing 186 feet above them, or to teeter on the huge jetty rocks. From a berm of drift logs, close by their cars, a few notice me as I bump ashore. I dump the water off my spray skirt and rise up and out of my cockpit before the next wave turns my boat. As my kayak lifts, I bring her higher up. From a line of flotsam I can see the tide has turned and I begin to laugh. "That was not mom taking you to school," I think. "That was daddy taking you over his knee."

As I lay my dry bags on weathered logs, I breathe out long and slow, thinking over the strangeness of this journey. I have covered a little over two hundred river miles between Vernita Bridge and this beach, a trip few paddlers ever take, opting for more exotic or more exciting destinations. In my opinion, trips rarely get as interesting as the Columbia, with its ever-changing scenery, atomic sentinels, enchanted islands, drowned history, bohemian backwaters, metropolitan cities, rain-shrouded towns, and engineered parks. I realize this has been my own paddle of discovery—no match for the experience of Lewis and Clark, but it is with a growing humility toward the spirit of this river as it leaps out from our constraints that I too can still call the Columbia "this great river."

~~~

For Immediate Release, November 5, 1999:
"President Clinton today announced an expansion of a wildlife refuge at the Department of Energy's Hanford Site in southeastern Washington State that will protect prime salmon habitat along the Columbia River."

Six months after I paddled the Hanford Reach, this quiet announcement marked a reprieve for the fall Chinook salmon that spawn on the Reach. It ensured a chance for survival for the more than sixty new-to-science plants and insect species discovered on the uplands that flank this still wild part of the Columbia. For the paddlers, jet boat users, fishers, hunters, and birders alike that love the Reach in its natural state, this Executive Order is a victory in preserving the lone free-flowing stretch of the Columbia River and the eastern Washington wilderness that surrounds it. Now the way is clear for the Hanford Reach of the Columbia to be designated as a Wild and Scenic River.

GUNKHOLING

◆

The Oregon and California Coasts

GUNKHOLING is a recreational sailor's term for exploring a coastline. The word implies an unplanned itinerary and a surplus of time. It can aptly describe sea kayaking between Northern California and the mouth of the Columbia River. Kayaking on this coast is gunkholing by car along Highway 101, putting in where the shore gets interesting and the weather permits.

THE LOST COAST: Strong Breezes

"Dairy Queen, Buck."

"Buck" is Will Cooper's all-purpose nickname for any or all of us. The Dairy Queen is his link with the road-trip world. Slowed by the thirty-mile-an-hour speed limit of the gas and fast food strip in Grants Pass, Oregon, our one-car, three-kayak caravan turns into the drive-in's parking lot. We step out into the ninety-five-degree heat of a southwestern Oregon August day.

Will orders a large "Oreo Blizzard"—a sort of solidified milkshake with crumbled Oreo cookies throughout. Cam Broze and I stand in the shade (we ordered the smaller version), failing in the heat to arrive at some disparaging remark on Will's penchant for this multicalorie concoction. "I eat anything on the road," Will had mentioned at our first Dairy Queen stop outside of Olympia, Washington—at ten in

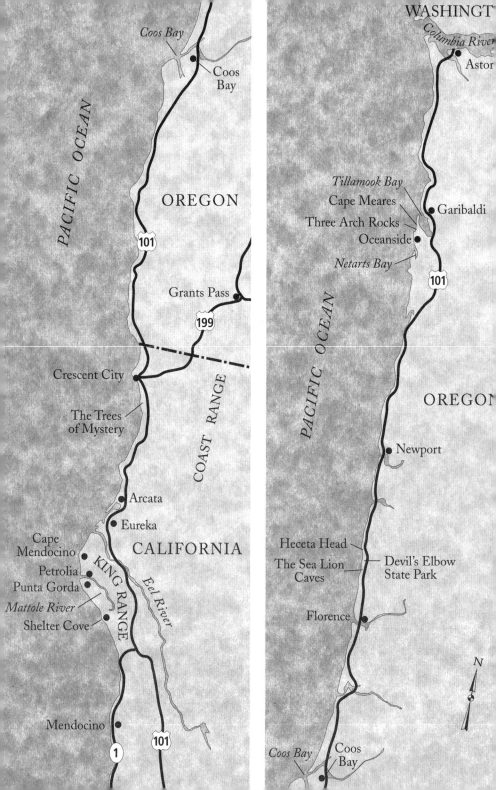

the morning. We old men in the shade nod knowingly to our younger friend with the body fat percentage on a par with dietary yogurt. His time for moderation in road-food dining will come soon enough. We check the kayak tie-downs on the Volvo, pile back in the car, and regain speed westbound on Oregon State Highway 199 through the first of the Coast Range redwood forests.

Cam, the codesigner of Mariner Kayaks with his brother Matt, and Will, a professional massage therapist, are serious sea kayakers who believe they will paddle all the coast that's worth paddling in their time. Today's twelve-hour, three–Dairy Queen drive is a true test of such dedication. But our first destination is such a curiosity, the name alone is enough to get us past Grants Pass. We are going to paddle the Lost Coast, so named by the descendants of the sheep ranchers and timber men who one hundred years ago effectively fought the encroachment of roads and people. The Lost Coast remains the last unpopulated, roadless wilderness coast of Northern California.

South of the Oregon-California border and west of the junction of Highways 1 and 101 lie over four hundred square miles of little-known terrain with sixty miles of rugged seashore—a region of California that has remained rural to wild. Few have visited it; far fewer have ever paddled it.

As we wind out of the Coast Range at Crescent City and join Highway 101, it appears there's a good chance it will stay that way: fog blots our first view of the Pacific. The Lost Coast, like most west coast capes and headlands that breast the Pacific, is excessively rich in wind and weather. From the Columbia River south, the summer coast is swaddled in fog, the capes are windy—constantly windy—and it is decidedly cooler than Grants Pass. We travel south through Arcata and Eureka, subdued by the grey sky and the possibility that fog and wind will keep us on the beach tomorrow. We're 594 miles out of Seattle, some thirteen miles south of Eureka, when we leave 101 and cross the Eel River, which marks the boundary of the Lost Coast.

I had been here before—trying to paddle the Lost Coast the previous September and failing because of similar weather conditions. As we drive the remaining forty miles through the fog-shrouded ranchlands, I can smell the sweat of the tall meadow grasses blending with the salt of the sea. It is a California of yesteryear, dusty brown grasslands, rolling hills, evergreens in the draws, a few cattle, a long strip of deserted beach without a human trace. Climbing to one last summit, we drive the long, winding downgrade into the town of Petrolia.

Petrolia is not much more than a bend in the road—fifty people call it home. Its simple wood-frame houses, church, and school are sited on a bench beside the Mattole River in a beautiful yellow-green valley of meadows, glades, and forested hills. But this forgotten town has a ghost in the backyard: hinted at by its name, Petrolia is the birthplace of the California oil industry. It was just two miles north of here that the first producing oil well in California was drilled and, in 1865, the first shipment of one hundred goatskins of crude oil was packed out by mule train.

Mercifully, Petrolia was no Prudhoe Bay. There are no oil wells remaining, and there are no Dairy Queens. The only people drifting through are campers heading for the county beach five and a half miles west, which is our put-in for the Lost Coast.

We arrive in the dark. Our headlights reveal several tents rustling in the breeze. We stop short of miring the Volvo in sand, and settle for an exposed campsite.

Cam with characteristic understatement notes that it's a bit breezy. We climb through a barrier of driftlogs meant to keep motor vehicles from driving on the beach and follow the sound of the surf down to the hard sand. Though the surf is a slight two to four feet high, it is coming in on a steep beach and breaking suddenly right where a kayaker would enter the water. "Windy, too," says Will. Wind this late at night is not a good sign for tomorrow. We walk back and bivouac beside the car, as a chilly night settles over the mouth of the Mattole River.

I rise at dawn, cold and stiff, to see what the conditions are offshore. The wind is still blowing, ten knots or more, roughing up the surface of the sea, darkening the crests of the swells. The fog has moved away from the beach and lies a mile offshore, a one-thousand-foot-high white wall highlighted with a touch of sunrise pink, stretching from Cape Mendocino to Punta Gorda. I stroll an immense sweep of grey-brown sand bermed with tufts of dune grass along its higher margin. This is the bay-mouth beach of the Mattole River, an environment pocked with the footprints of yesterday's wanderers.

By the time I turn and go with the wind it is whitecapping out past the break, and I realize the Lost Coast is going to stymie me again. Back at camp, after each of us has hiked out past the beach logs and pondered the wind, the fog bank, the surf, and the thirty miles of open coast to Shelter Cove, we decide not to go.

At 8:00 A.M. there are just too many cautions. We don't like the fog—we could paddle in it, but it's no fun paddling in a vacuum. The wind will probably increase throughout the day, building the wind waves and creating the potential for a difficult surf landing on an unscouted beach. And to make matters official, we have the warning from the *Coast Pilot*, the mariner's point-by-point, reef-by-shoal encyclopedia of current information on local weather, seas, unusual conditions, and navigation for all U.S. coastal waters. For the Pacific Coast, its terse prose describes Punta Gorda, on our intended route, two miles south:

> *A high, bold, rounding cape 11 miles south of Cape Mendocino, the seaward face rising to about 900 feet (Punta Gorda) is bare of trees, except in the gulches. The grey rectangular structure of an*

abandoned lighthouse, 25 feet high, is south of the point. For over 1.5 miles north and 2.0 miles south of the point, the beach is bordered by numerous rocks and shoals extending in some cases 0.6 mile offshore.

The wind, sea, and currents off Punta Gorda are probably as strong as off any given point on the coast; frequent and strong tide rips have been noted. Many times when the weather at Shelter Cove is clear and calm and the sea smooth, both the wind and the sea will pick up as Punta Gorda is approached, until just north of this point where strong breezes to moderate gales will be experienced. At other times clear weather south of this point will lead to fog north, or vice versa.

"Or vice versa." Silently eating our granola, we are wondering if we should attempt to do it, but the boats stay lashed to the Volvo. To salvage something from our decision and see what we can of the coast, Cam mentions being curious about the Punta Gorda lighthouse, abandoned back in 1951, and we decide to hike to it. The downwind leg is through low dunes and past fenced Mattole Indian archaeological digs. At times we walk the beach, dodging the swash of the waves, watching the reefs and the sea beyond. At one point there is a perfect bay formed by the low reefs that is not apparent on the topographic maps. It would allow a safe, even dry, landing. Cam comments that at a higher tide and with a heavier sea, the waves would sweep right into this bay. Nonetheless I keep watching the possible route around the point, aching at the proper but frustrating decision not to paddle. And still the wind increases.

When we reach Punta Gorda, we decide to climb up over the grassy ridge. We spook cattle out of the sheltered gulches and watch the chilly return of the fog. Before we can walk the remaining half-mile to the squat little lighthouse, the wind begins tearing the tops off the breaking waves.

Back at our car, we follow Highway 101 north into Oregon, out of the wind, gunkholing up the highway of kitsch.

HECETA HEAD: Roadside Attraction

Highway 101, the "Redwood Highway," is the home of burlwood tables, myrtlewood bowls, and redwood trees, the Trees of Mystery, Trees of Confusion, and the Tour-Thru-Tree, the world's tallest totem pole, the world's shortest river, Twenty Miracle Miles of craft shops, Tillamook Cheese, and the Sea Lion Caves. The Sea Lion Caves, a tourist site featuring a fifteen-hundred-foot-long sea cave filled with honking, barking sea lions, are just north of Florence, Oregon. This one attraction must consume one-third of the state's pulp tree production just to maintain the prolific bumper sticker marketing. We have seen the bumper ads our entire trip, but now in the afternoon of our third day, 171 miles into Oregon, they are coming thick and fast.

Highway 101 has left the dunes above Coos Bay, rising with the basalt cliffs that form Heceta Head. As 101 narrows, hugging the cliff, cars and campers brush by one another, everyone straining to get a new perspective on the ocean breaking below. It is here, just beyond Sea Lion Caves, that the most famous Kodak picture point of the Oregon coast commands people to careen their cars into the turnouts. The photographer of each family becomes quite serious and stands into the wind, aiming his or her camera toward Heceta Head, its lighthouse commanding a craggy promontory, the surf exploding beneath it. We are no different. The view is timeless and evocative. As we continue along the precipice, signs for Devil's Elbow State Park begin to slip by. At the entrance to the park, we drive down to a cove, some polite surf, and one of the best paddles on the Oregon coast.

There is something so satisfying about dragging your kayak across the sand to the water's edge, putting on your spray skirt and life jacket, and paddling away from the last dry margins of shore. Each and every time I get into a kayak and quickly travel out to where, as a child, I never expected to be, I feel a personal excitement that strengthens my strokes and drives my kayak through the swells.

One by one we negotiate the surf, which is not more than three feet high in this protected bay. Will takes a couple of waves over the bow that drench him. Cam and I miss the breakers by weaving through a hole in the surf line caused by the uneven ocean bottom. If you want to get away from a beach dry, as many of us do, there are ways. If you read a beach, watch the break, find its weakness, sense the rhythm of the wave sets—you just might do it. At Devil's Elbow, as the swell comes ashore it "feels" the bottom, and its friction slows and steepens the waves until they break.

Cam and I head for a deeper area of the cove. Here the approaching waves continue on without breaking for an extra fifteen or twenty yards, while the same waves on either side rush in over shallower water, break, and slow. We scoot through the resulting gap and paddle quickly to beat the next wave, dry as a bone. A sputtering Will is out beyond the shore break, and we wait while he repairs the damage. I scan a hazy sky and an almost windless sea. What a difference a new day, a few hundred miles, and a less exposed cape make.

We can run north or south. Either direction is not a long paddle— about a mile and a half. But the headland, this gigantic set of rock buttresses splaying into the sea, riddled with caves and arches, lures us to explore. Without much further conversation, we decide to head north through a small arch that opens to a cave in one direction and a safe exit in the other. The Heceta Head lighthouse flashes 205 feet above us, a million-candlepower beam visible for twenty miles.

One by one we negotiate a narrow pass, a channel of confused sea; first Cam, then Will, then I. We try to establish whether there is a reef below us by paddling in place, watching a big set of waves move through, and scrutinizing the passing crests for anything solid visible in the trough. We play follow-the-leader through the rock gardens for the next hour. When we reach the end of the headland, we turn and retrace our path, running the gauntlets and arches until we stand off Sea Lion Caves. We look up at the tourists a good three hundred feet above us staring down.

The cave is amazing: it is actually a huge tunnel with a cavernous, chambered opening to the south and a smaller portal through the headland to the north. A prodigious number of Steller's sea lions have taken shelter here for thousands of years. We can't go in the cave—it's the sea lions' domain. We also keep well back from the outer rock ledges, so we do not spook the animals. Approaching the end of the cliffs, we turn in unison, paddling together in continued good weather. For a moment I wonder what's happening at Punta Gorda, but that is for another time, another attempt.

"Dairy Queen, Buck!"

CAPE MEARES: Three Arch Rocks

Why is it that the average Oregon coast restaurant seems to be intent on thickening its clam chowder to the consistency of bread dough? Each year I travel the highways, the chowder gets a little thicker: crackers are superfluous, steak knives an eventual necessity. Poor Will. Poor me. I also subscribe to Will's precept of eating anything I want to on the road: chicken-fried steaks, caramel milk shakes, Denver omelets. Will is incorrigible—he orders onion rings so deep-fat-fried you can hardly find the onion. The Oreo Blizzard is a veritable health food by comparison.

· THE HIDDEN COAST ·

After traveling north to Cape Meares, covering much of the 374-mile length of Oregon's part of Highway 101, we stop at the town of Garibaldi and pull up at a seafood restaurant. During our meal, Will and I discuss the relative merits of a chain or franchise restaurant versus the mom-and-pop drive-in. It's tough these days to find anything along the road worth eating. There seem to be numerous trends, none of them good, to my mind. The most obvious is that the McDonalds and Dairy Queens are forcing the small-town mom-and-pop drive-ins out of business. As they struggle, the small diners have cut corners to the extent that you can hardly trust the egg on your plate. Along 101, there is a steady disappearance of real food: you're offered nondairy creamers, fake butter, and imitation sour cream—a true sacrilege. Ice cream is made from a mix, hamburgers are laced with vegetable filler, and everything is either salted or sugared into inedibility.

My clam chowder stares back without a response. Will is having french fries and gravy. We are losing daylight and have yet to find a campsite. After we beg a photocopy of the local chart from the Coast Guard, we pilot the Volvo out to Cape Meares. In the dark and the fog, we camp beside a back road. The following morning, we drive to our put-in on the southern side of the cape, at the beach town of Oceanside.

Cape Meares is flanked on either side by saltwater lagoons; the larger to the north is called Tillamook Bay, the smaller is Netarts Bay. Cape Meares would do Ireland's coast proud. Vertical cliffs to 640 feet isolate a series of bays and caves for two miles. And off the cliffs, a half-mile out to sea, Three Arch Rocks promises new paddling adventures.

Our put-in is a small cove on the southern, protected (in summer) side of a large point. As at Heceta Head, the waves are three feet, and we ride out on what must be a riptide channel to the Arches. There we encounter some of the most monumental deepwater architecture we've seen.

· GUNKHOLING ·

What strikes you about Three Arch Rocks is that they have their own kind of symmetry. The first passage is one hundred feet long and forty feet high, the second one hundred feet high and forty feet long. The third arch is so like a major freeway tunnel you'd swear it had been engineered: one hundred feet long, sixty feet wide, forty feet high, and straight as an arrow. In all three, there are no visible reefs, no jutting buttresses or side caverns, just hundreds of whitewashed perches for birds: pigeon guillemots, a charcoal-colored seabird with white wing bars and flashy red feet; common murres, the species that was the most impacted by the *Exxon Valdez* spill; and, though not in the caves but nesting nearby and fishing just off my bow, the tufted puffin, the rare little racer of the seas, always seen with several little fish sandwiched in its beak.

Paddling around these islets, it is obvious that every nook, ledge, lee, and even the wind-exposed northern sides of these rocks are life-giving sanctuaries. Gulls predominate, and pelicans also gather here. Cormorants line the crowns of the rocks closer to the water, and sea lions by the hundreds bark in casual alarm.

As long as I do not approach too close and cause a sea-lion-pup-flattening stampede, I can edge into their presence, usually drawing forth a few younger males to sniff me out. If you are downwind from their perch, the animals will try to get downwind of you, making long drawn-out snorts. About ten youngsters, long necks craning, come out of the water to their shoulders, bunching behind me and vying for the spot that gives the strongest whiff of my scent. They bark in what must be a pungent chorus of sea lion tunes but cause no alarm. I allow the drift of the current to pull me away from their rocks.

I race to catch up with Will and Cam as they approach the main part of the headland. From cove to cove, we check for reefs and then paddle in. As the waves steepen and roll beneath us, each swell sends a breeze past us seaward, reminding me of the wild ride off Shi Shi Beach. I wonder if my alertness to danger has improved since that episode. But there will be no rogue waves today, just perfect arches and an occasional puffin flying by like a giant bee. Cam is anxious to try some surfing back at the Oceanside beach, so we turn for the surfing and inevitable dunking and home.

ANACAPA CROSSING

The Santa Barbara Channel Islands

THE HOUSES EDGING the Santa Barbara Channel are going for nothing less than a million. At Oxnard, a breakwater has been added and a dense canalside development fills the harbor. Just past the suburbanized Coast Guard station lies a small public beach, unadorned except for a line of cormorants atop the breakwater, wings hung out to dry.

I pull my car to a stop and become a player entering the rhythm of the Southern California dawn: trim runners in neon spandex jog by wired to their Walkmans; gardeners' pickups pass en route to their first appointments, clean, waxed, and unhurried. The waterway is already active with pleasure craft skipping out on another fine, sunny Friday—everyone here expects good weather as if it is a right. The Southern California mystique pervades even this last remaining strip of undeveloped shore.

Not knowing whether I'm an anachronism or the wave of the California boating future, I heft my kayak to join the group bound for Anacapa Island. Between trips from the car to the beach, I meet the other paddlers; we exchange names and size each other up. We are five men and one woman, ranging in ages from twenty-eight to fifty-four.

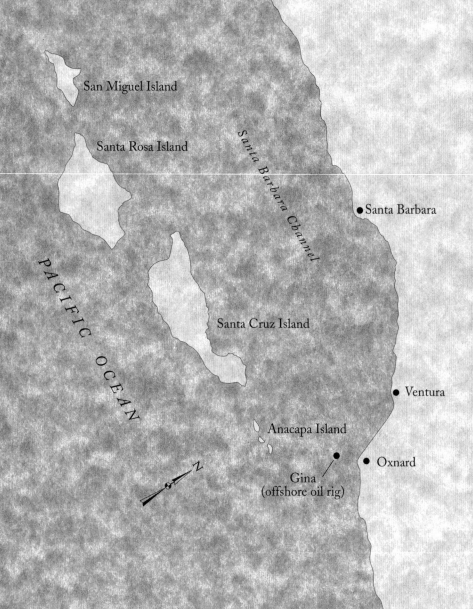

CALIFORNIA

San Miguel Island

Santa Rosa Island

Santa Barbara Channel

●Santa Barbara

PACIFIC OCEAN

Santa Cruz Island

●Ventura

Anacapa Island

●Oxnard

Gina
(offshore oil rig)

N

· ANACAPA CROSSING ·

Richard and Mark are engineers, Peter sells for a multinational printing firm. Our guides are Joanne Turner and Doug Schwartz, owners of Southwind Kayak Center. Both appear to be at ease with the group, the weather, and the crossing.

Doug calls us together and outlines the three-day trip: our destination is Anacapa, one of the smallest of the eight Channel Islands and one of four islands that comprise the Channel Islands National Park. The name of the island is derived from the native Chumash word *eneeapah,* meaning "deception." Anacapa is just that—it is one of nature's stage props. Just over three miles long, the island looks large on the ocean horizon, its highest hill nearly a thousand feet. But in reality, Anacapa is three joined islets and averages only a third of a mile in width. Trending west, it is dwarfed by nearby Santa Cruz Island with ninety-six square miles, Santa Rosa Island with eighty-four square miles, and fourteen-square-mile San Miguel Island. Together, the four form the northern chain of islands that enclose Santa Barbara Channel.

Today we will paddle the thirteen miles across the channel to camp on Anacapa, and the following day we will circumpaddle the island. On Sunday, weather permitting, we'll paddle back. Steady winds rising in the afternoon, ship traffic, possible fog, and lots of exercise are in store for us. Joanne goes over the safety factors: we learn a basic set of hand signals, and we are cautioned to stay together and wear our life jackets at all times on the water.

As I listen to Joanne and Doug, I like the way these two have put the trip together—it will be safe, because of their local knowledge, judgment, and skill, and the fact that they require all of us to have ocean and surf experience, and simple, with each of us being responsible for his own food and kit. Then Joanne and Doug, unlike most outfitters, actually will have time to share the relaxing aspects of the trip. We finish loading, don life jackets, and shove off.

This is to be a long crossing: Doug anticipates about three hours of open ocean paddling. This morning, it's sun at our backs, light winds on our right cheek, and a four-foot westerly swell. Free of the traffic at the jetty entrance, I paddle with the pleasant satisfaction of once again being on the sea. My shadow runs ahead of me across a deeply blue approaching wave, as my Polaris settles into the trough with little fuss. The sea surface is busy but there's no spray, and my apprehension about the big crossing, bad weather, and new people drops away with every stroke.

Joanne lets out a sharp "whoop" for attention, then points at a big smudge on the horizon known as "Gina," Unocal's offshore oil rig, four miles out to sea. In line with distant and not yet visible Anacapa, Gina is our fixed navigational aid for the next hour, our compass heading that in time tells us we are drifting south. Doug calls a course change, pointing us in a more northerly direction, and then settles back to talk to me, paddle-to-paddle, about the risks of kayaking to the Channel Islands.

"The wind averages seventeen to twenty-one knots in the spring— that's force five on the Beaufort scale, twenty-four hours a day," Doug says. "Wind waves can reach eight feet out here easily, on any afternoon. By summer, it tapers to the yearly average of eleven to sixteen knots, and September is a calm force three at seven to ten knots. That is pre- cisely what we've got this morning. But the real fear on this crossing is not the wind but the fog. All through the summer, fog can blanket this channel and we won't go. We'll sit on the beach until it lifts."

I wonder, "Why not use a compass?" And Doug answers my unasked question: "It's the ships that stop you. Over thirty big ships pass between Anacapa and Oxnard daily—container ships, tankers, and air- craft carriers—all moving at twenty to thirty knots. In the fog they are deadly. You can't hear one of those container ships on a collision course—they are absolutely silent."

And so are we. Two hours out, midway, we stop to let a bulk carrier sailing under a Greek flag pass at three hundred yards. There is no indication that the men on the bridge have seen us, as the ship rumbles by.

Morning turns to afternoon, and we are bow on to Anacapa. Cliffs ring the island. There are no beaches or safe harbors to speak of. Our eastern islet destination is meadowed, golden in the September sun. A lighthouse flashes on the closest promontory, and we paddle toward this vision.

The wind, slowly rising since mid-channel, has reached a steady fifteen to twenty knots. A strong set of sea waves with breaking crests moves in from the west, and we begin turning to meet the big ones. I check my paddling partners—everyone still has a smile. Richard gets slapped with a breaker and howls, as the seawater find its way beneath his spray skirt.

The lighthouse seems to be getting no closer. At first I think it's just the game of distance versus the desire to get there, but not more than two miles off Anacapa we discover we are virtually standing still. Joanne steams up, her bow clearing the crests to mid-coaming. She gives a yelp for attention and signals a turn to the west—into the wind and a current we had suspected since passing Gina but whose strength we'd had no idea of until now. At rest, we are being carried by the current past the southeast end of Anacapa at a good three knots. We paddle a hard hour toward the island in a ferry glide, using the wind to sail us like a close-hauled sailboat, until the rough sea and the bite of the current lessen in the shadow of Anacapa's cliffs.

We gather in a small, rounded bay, not more than 100 feet in diameter and rimmed on three sides by 150-foot-high cliffs. Our harbor is scant protection, the sea waves scudding by no more than three boat lengths away. We congratulate ourselves on our long, but exhilarating paddle; our muscles ring with their sudden stillness.

Landing at Anacapa is the next hurdle. There is no beach, no rocky reef—just walls of ancient lava rising to the sunlight. Doug and Richard have landed at a pier cemented to the west side of the rock and have grabbed a ladder and hauled themselves up to the deck. They throw down carabiners and rope rigged together as a rudimentary pulley system. Joanne hooks on my boat's bow and stern, and on a rising wave I grab the ladder and climb up, my boat hoisted up behind me.

The national park ranger descends the steep staircase to give us our orientation. He warns us about smoking, seeming surprised and pleased that no one does, and tells us about the island. Anacapa is the most visited of the four islands that make up Channel Islands National Park—one of the least visited parks in the nation. Since the days of the Spanish, man has looked to the Channel Islands for opportunity. The sea otters that once inhabited the area in abundance were hunted to extinction. The ironwood forests that filled the island's draws were cut. Goats were introduced, as well as sheep, cattle, horses, pigs, rabbits, and other environmental loose cannons. With most endemic species munched to oblivion, the denuded islands supported a few ranches and sheltered occasional hermits. They even acted as convenient targets for the military.

In 1938, the preciousness of these last wilderness islands, so close to but so distant from the burgeoning California culture, was recognized. Anacapa and the tiny, mile-square Santa Barbara of the southern Channel Islands were first designated a national monument. And in 1980, they became a national park, adding Santa Rosa and San Miguel Islands.

We thank the ranger for the information. One senses he and his family will not make a career out of lonely Anacapa, as the sound of his footfalls up the stairs is lost in the vigor of the wind.

The only campsites allowed on Anacapa are a third of a mile into the wind. To carry our gear up the 144 steps to the tablelike meadow, Joanne suggests we balance our drybags on our paddle shafts, and like coolies, we climb. Our designated home is in a slight depression in the ridge that forms the southern cliff edge. Contained by a rock-wall perimeter, the site has three picnic tables and two outhouses. We aim our tents into the wind and weight every corner with rocks. On the islands as well as the sea, the wind dominates, deals the day's plan, forms shelter in the lee, and wreaks danger to windward. It sweeps this dry island, sculpts the grasses of the meadows, and supports the hovering peregrine. It is no place to leave a dome tent unweighted.

Dinner will have to wait. Hungry as we are, the island has to be appreciated. Looking back over the meadow, past the Anacapa light-house and its twenty-four-hour foghorn, the mainland hills are blue in the distance, the channel flecked with whitecaps—most noticeably a mile off our island where we had experienced the biggest waves and strongest wind. To the west behind the ridge, the light of sunset draws us out. We follow a path along the ridge that is edged with rocks on either side to keep us from straying onto the fragile grasses—a signal of a new and caring stewardship for this little island.

Leaning into a buffeting wind, our eyes follow the knifelike ridge-lines of Anacapa's islets zigzagging toward the west. The sky is a pure yellow in the clean sunset air, the hills black in silhouette. Two ravens arc across the golden sky and drop below the cliff edge, to rise hovering almost within reach.

∼∼∼

The following morning, the wind I expected to be stilled rattles my tent. We brew coffee in the shelter of the outhouse—the only wind-break we can find. Within the hour, Doug and Joanne herd us toward our kayaks, the lifeboat-like put-in, and the circumnavigation of Anacapa.

· THE HIDDEN COAST ·

The same current we fought yesterday now scoots us around the eastern end of the island, through the picturesque arch that has become the symbol of the Channel Islands. Bathed in sun, rimmed by a filigree of pelicans, the arch resembles a natural, if slouching, Arc de Triomphe, standing free of the island among a number of smaller sea stacks and offshore reefs. Pelicans, cormorants, and gulls rise in complaint as we paddle under the arch and enter the quieter water on the south shore of the island.

It is as if the weather god flipped a switch—no wind. For twenty-four hours we have been leaning into the wind, cranking our voices up a notch just to be heard. Now it is so quiet we listen in awe. One by one we begin to strip off some layers of clothing, the heat of the sun now full force. As my kayak drifts among the floating kelp, I drag my hand in the remarkably clear water. Far below, a brilliant flash of red-gold sparks my curiosity. Doug thinks it can only be a garibaldi—a rockfish the color of a California poppy. I follow its movements through the kelp forest until it blurs from sight.

Secretly, I'm hoping a sea lion will pass beneath me; instead, the next critter is a human, a diver no doubt after the garibaldi. Ahead, the diveboat that brought the diver lies at anchor. We had seen the craft that morning, bucking into the same conditions we paddled through yesterday. It must have over twenty scuba divers aboard. Safe behind Anacapa, the black-and-blue-garbed divers flop happily into the sea.

We paddle past their stares. One diver asks if we had paddled over, and we nod—John Wayne could not have done it better. I can't help but think of the Aleuts, who made the crossing in half the time.

In a brief and unusual period of California history, the Aleuts of the Aleutian Islands once hunted off the Channel Islands. Beginning in 1807 with an agreement between the Russian-American Company's Alexander Andreivich Baranov and one Joseph O'Cain of Boston,

· ANACAPA CROSSING ·

Aleut hunters with their sea kayaks—baidarkas as the Russians called them—were loaded aboard O'Cain's ships and brought 1,700 miles south from Alaska to hunt the sea otter.

Never had the hunters seen so many otters, defenseless against the numbers of men, the small swift kayaks, and the barbed bone lances. In the ensuing years, the ships of Boston would mother fleets of Aleut kayakers to hunt from Trinidad, which was near the present-day border of California and Oregon, to the Baja California peninsula. It was a headlong slaughter. There was no thought of conservation. And there is no record of the Aleuts, who were conscripts at best—almost no mention of them at all. One of the few European comments about the Aleut hunters states that they took to the hunt "like the eager dog at the sight of game." In three years, 1809 through 1811, for example, over eight thousand sea otters were taken within San Francisco Bay alone, by fleets of over 140 sea kayaks.

Today, there are no sea otters at Anacapa. No one knows when the last one was killed—most likely, around 1900. The Monterey sea otter community, one of the only groups to survive the hunt, has rebounded to 2,090 individuals as of April 1999. In 1987, a translocation community of twenty sea otters was established on San Nicolas Island, forty-four miles due south of Anacapa. Today this relocation effort has been adandoned, due in part to the pressure of competing fishermen. Now the otters are expanding their range naturally, perhaps one day to return to the protective kelp beds of the Channel Islands.

∿

Paddling at an unhurried pace, we continue our circumpaddle, we are tailed by harbor seals instead of otters, and flying fish break the surface off our bows. Rounding the western tip of Anacapa, we expect to encounter the wind but are surprised instead by light air and a subdued sea. Doug is excited as he dons his helmet; we should have safe access to the cave-riddled northern coast.

The helmet is worn to cushion your head in case you get, as Doug calls it, "squeezed" against the roof of a cave by an invading wave. I strap the helmet provided by Southwind Kayak to my head, with appreciation. It's one thing to paddle into a dark cave beneath the weight of a rock and lava ceiling. But to float to the top of a marine cave and be pressed there like some cartoon character—this is the stuff of nightmares.

We paddle through the afternoon from cave to cave. Some are fractures with long, narrow entries; others are big enough to moor a sailboat in. There are tunnels and chambers, bends and turns in complete darkness. Others are like grottos painted with the colors of the sea. At each entrance, we watch the wave patterns and edge in one at a time. We move slowly, watching for hidden reefs and the sudden appearance of cave-dwelling cormorants. Doug goes first and Joanne takes up the rear, as we poke in and out of the underpinnings of Anacapa.

Doug and Joanne pause beneath a majestic cliff rising about two hundred feet. Past the kelp beds at its base a small opening is visible, protected by a perimeter of rocks and reefs. Doug pulls us together and explains: "This is what we call Cathedral Cave. You start by skirting the rocks, and once inside you follow me through a narrow corridor that opens to a set of chambers beneath the mass of the headland. There are three exits over on the other side of the point—all in safe water. Ready?"

One glance back past the rocks at a Maxfield Parrish scene of brilliant sun on alabaster sea stacks rising from an ultramarine sea, and then I ride a mild swell into the darkness. Mayhem—my eyes dilating, I strain to see my surroundings, floating on a surging river of seawater. At times the passage is too cramped to paddle and I fend off the walls of what appears to be more like a mine shaft than a cave. Ahead, Richard is in white water. The waves that had passed ahead of him now rebound from the side chambers in a vision that would make Indiana Jones wince. A moment later I am caught in waves coming from three sides; my kayak rises and I automatically duck my head. I look up and realize I've passed through the corridor and into a grand chamber. I sweep to the left and wait as Joanne comes busting through, wide-eyed. One by one, we gather in a space perhaps one hundred feet across. A filtered and refracted light from the three passages to the outside illuminates mosque-like vaulted ceilings tiled in lavender algae and rimmed by pale-green anemones and purple sea urchins. It is as wonderful a world as I've ever seen—a kayakers-only paradise. I linger until claustrophobia gets to me, and then I squeeze out into the soft light of the late afternoon.

We finish our long day of exploring, experiencing some of the most difficult and enchanting sea kayaking of our lives, conscious of the impact we have had on these beleaguered islands. Wilderness such as Cathedral Cave is an eroding entity in California, existing only in the inaccessible. Our kayaks are so suited to exploring the hidden parts of the coast—and yet, it is sometimes difficult to accept our presence here.

We continually surprise an already weary wildlife on our return to camp. Doug cautions me from paddling too close to shore because there are sea lions around the next stack, and I change course without question. I'd like to think the self-actualizing nature of our sport creates an affinity with and an understanding of the wild places we explore. Although it is naive to think wisdom comes with the kayak and paddle, as our kayaking community grows we must honor and protect the rights of those living things we come in contact with.

Again we hoist the boats and take the hike back to camp in time for sunset. We will be gone in the morning.

THE
TRANSLUCENT SEA

◆

Baja and the Sea of Cortez

Everything concerning Baja California is of such little importance
that it is hardly worth the trouble to take a pen and write about it.
Of poor shrubs, useless thorn bushes and bare rocks, of miles of
sand without water and wood . . . what shall I or can I report?

—Johann Jakob Baeger, S.J., 1772

Stripped hills, cold volcano, stone and hot wind under all that
splendor, drought, the taste of dust, a barefoot sound in the dust
and a pepper tree in the midst of desert like a petrified fountain!

—Octavio Paz, 1963

BY MID-NOVEMBER, the first winter storms strike across western
Wyoming with freezing, sidecut winds and heavy snow. The Seattle
papers usually carry a wire-service piece telling which cities were hardest
hit. I always read this first winter report to see whether it mentions
Lander, Wyoming. For Lander is the home of Charles Fiala, former
director of the National Outdoor Leadership School, my onetime
roommate, and the friend who introduced me to both sea kayaking

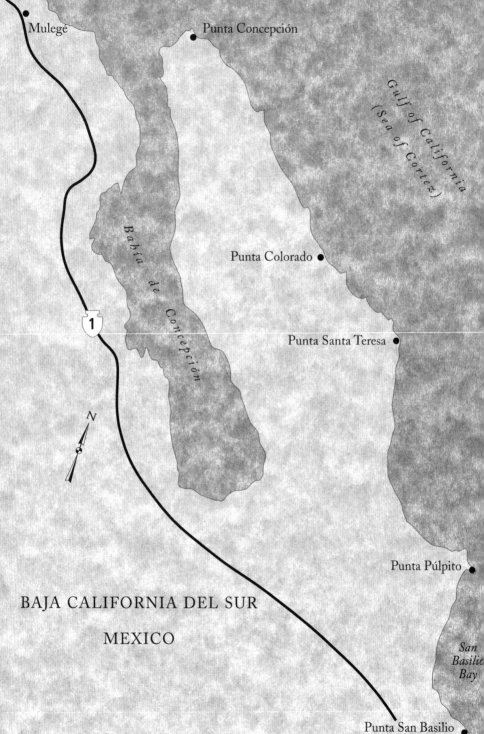

Mulegé

Punta Concepción

Gulf of California
(Sea of Cortez)

Punta Colorado

Bahía de Concepción

1

Punta Santa Teresa

N

Punta Púlpito

BAJA CALIFORNIA DEL SUR

MEXICO

San
Basilio
Bay

Punta San Basilio

Caleta de San Juanico
(San Juanico Cove)

and Baja California. It usually takes one good storm, maybe two, to hit Lander before Charley digs himself out, calls me, and we begin planning our sometimes annual rendezvous south of the border.

We toss around dates and people: Standish from San Francisco, Chris Johnson out of Ketchum. Sarah's finals are over on the tenth, Fran has a commitment on March 2. Dracos and Patty can put us up in San Diego. Charley suggests that we take the "northern route," a classic paddle along the east coast of Baja. We set a date for mid-February, and assign group gear among those who are coming. Now we can accept winter's worst with the anticipation of remote coasts and guaranteed sun.

About twenty-five million years ago, Baja California slowly began to separate from the Mexican mainland. At a rate geologists estimate to be an inch a year, the entire land mass has traveled 450 miles to the north and west, causing the Gulf of California to form behind it. This intervening body of water, once called the Sea of Cortez, insulated the plant and animal populations, the indigenous people, and Father Johann Jakob Baeger for that matter, on a remnant of land 800 miles long and not more than 100 miles wide.

Baja is a volcanic landscape, the color of ochre and rust, the composition of sediment, ash, and lava. Beneath its overburden of volcanic soils lie ancient sea beds, fossilized rhododendrons, tropical vegetation, even twenty-ton duck-billed dinosaurs. Man has only scratched the surface—at Tijuana, La Paz, and Cabo San Lucas. The rest of the land is thinly settled, isolated, and quixotic beneath clear skies, flanked by warm seas, strewn with mountains, mesas, arroyos, and plains.

Our two-car caravan is five hundred miles south of Tijuana on Highway 1, the only road that runs the length of the Baja peninsula. The guaranteed sun we had yearned for shimmers off the two-lane blacktop. Oncoming vehicles, miles distant across the flat landscape called the Vizcaino Desert, are dissolved into caricature in the heat, then loom closer, solidify, and pass with a roar.

The entire interior of our car is coated with a fine dust, the air we breathe is hot, and our consumption of liquids is constant. By mid-afternoon we turn east, the highway curving around streams of red, geologically recent lava flows. We pass mute cinder cones and then the road, flanked by dented and twisted guardrails, drops with a twelve-percent grade to the relative cool of the coast.

The first sight of the Sea of Cortez rivets road-weary minds—an intense blue sea, streaked with whitecaps in stark contrast to the dry land. We sidle along the water's edge, heading south past Santa Rosalía's ancient, still-active copper mines, past the many roadside shrines commemorating bad luck on the narrow, seacliff road. Within an hour, our dusty automobiles pull into the remarkably tropical town of Mulegé, a seventeenth-century Spanish settlement sited along a palm-lined river. Charley guides us to a *mercado* to obtain the essentials of a true Baja expedition: limes, small cans of Heredez hot sauce, potent garlic and onions, fresh tortillas, and water—gallons of water.

Our put-in is a small mangrove-lined bay just south of town, which is overrun each year with an increasing number of RVs. Amid the satellite dishes and the open shelters with palm-frond roofs, we unload across the beach, sorting gear—each of us focusing on our individual load plans. After the last items are coerced behind seats or strapped on top of our decks, we gather to look at the route.

With the point of his knife, Charley traces our route on the old nautical chart of the Golfo de California from the USS *Narragansett* surveys of 1873 and 1875. The blade crosses three miles of open water from Mulegé to Punta Concepción and then edges south down the east side of a long, roadless peninsula. Cutting into places Charley has visited and named during his years as director of the National Outdoor

Leadership School's (NOLS) Baja branch, he describes the "aquarium," "lobster cove," and "plant place." For seventy miles, we will follow the route pioneered by the school over twenty years ago when "Tap" Tappley first brought the beamy Folbots south from Lander. Charley's rising excitement is infectious; we've got fourteen days to take our time, staying longer at the magic camps, moving when the weather allows.

Weather plays a background theme on every Baja trip. The gulf is a windy place, with wind enough to hold experienced kayakers in camp for days; hence the built-in extra time in our schedule. This morning it's calm and cloudless, which doesn't amount to a hill of *frijoles* anywhere along this coast. In winter, the wind blows from the north without clouds and without warning. Our policy will be to follow NOLS's long-established predawn starts, to paddle through the calm early hours into the glorious sunrise until wind or destination takes us ashore. Charley closes his knife with a snap. We turn to our boats and the last bit of packing; we're now down to the delicate use of full body weight to close hatches.

A Baja trip means a full boat: lots of toys for fishing, snorkeling, and pictures. The unfamiliar environment demands a library of books on birds, plants, fish, and the stars. Two weeks of food becomes a thirty-five-pound duffle bag. Charley had said on our first trip, many years ago, "If you don't get a wetsuit, you don't go. It's fifty percent of the trip." Ever since, I've packed a wetsuit top, weight belt, mask, snorkel, booties, and fins—all but the tanks and BCD (breathing control device). Special Baja items include a sun tarp, a grill, clothes for the chill of evening, and a goodly supply of aloe vera for sunburn. On top of all that, five gallons of water are needed—enough for six to eight hot days. We drag our boats to the cool waters of the Bahía de Concepción. My kayak is so heavy it has a momentum of its own, as I point east toward the slow mountainous rise of Punta Concepción.

· THE HIDDEN COAST ·

From previous trips comes the memory of our first camp, "the aquarium," seven miles distant. Just over the raised, flat headland that protects the landing lies a white sand beach—white sand blending to the color of the sea. I have been thinking of this one beach ever since Charley's call, imagining the infinite gradations of the sea's color from the palest lime stretching to an infinite series of deepening greens and azures and on to blues, my torso plunging into the wet world, fish scattering in silver surprise. John Steinbeck wrote about the Sea of Cortez in 1941:

> *The sea here swarms with life, and probably the ocean bed is equally rich. Microscopically, the water is crowded with plankton. This is the tuna water–life water. It is complete from plankton to gray porpoises. . . . There was food everywhere. Everything ate everything else with a furious exuberance.*

Now I hover just beneath the surface, tossed by the swell sweeping in above me. My body is pulled toward the reef, then released as the wave passes in a swirl of sunlit bubbles. The fins give me a speed so unlike swimming that I squirrel around the lagoon in bursts of joy. In the clefts and pockets of the reef, tiny fish watch as if curious, their little mouths working, their fins stabilizing iridescent bodies suspended in a translucent sea.

Beyond the reef, I launch out over a sea cliff. Twenty feet below is a series of long lava fingers running outward from the beach. Between them are lanes of sand, white carpets where only the hunters swim. I look for the rays—stingrays—vague diamond shapes concealed there.

In the dim blue distance, my vivid imagination conjures sharks. But they *are* sharks, gliding effortlessly on the edge of my vision. As they come closer, I realize with relief that they are only three or four feet long. Just as elegant and sleek as their parents, the trio of sharks with eerie eyes and a predator's urgency swim past, perhaps searching for the cabrilla, a delicate white fish Charley prefers for our favorite Baja appetizer *ceviche*—raw cabrilla marinated in lime juice, garlic, and salsa. I return to the surface, grab a deep breath, and instinctively submerge to search them out again—they are gone. Getting chilled and hungry, I swim back through the reef to our wind-protected cove and a welcome first night's dinner: *ceviche*, lobster, beans and rice, cornbread, coffee, and walnut pie.

In Baja, rain falls as if by lottery. One place may go for a year without a drop, while a neighboring valley is green with excess. But excess seldom means more than five inches a year—all in two or three torrential downpours. Baja is a land of stress and adaptation, as Joseph Wood Krutch describes in his book *Baja California and the Geography of Hope*:

> *In desert country everything from the color of a mouse or the shape of a leaf up to the largest features of the mountains themselves is more likely than not to have the same explanation: dryness. So far as living things go, all this adds up to what even an ecologist may so far forget himself as to call an "unfavorable environment." But like all such pronouncements this one doesn't mean much unless we ask "unfavorable for what and for whom?"*

At every new landing, once we've set up camp and gone for a welcome swim, the arroyo beckons. As a rule, our camps are on a beach formed by the outwash of the dry creek beds, or arroyos, that cut through the coastline to the sea. The curiosity of what lies up the arroyo begins with what at first appears to be a road—a country lane drawing me past giant cardon cacti. But it is actually a meticulously neat streambed curving back and forth between steep, matching hillsides.

When it rains, a hard-driving rain, this quiet canyon path is transformed into a chocolate-colored, boulder-carrying, flood-stage river. In the subsiding violence, sand sloughing from the hillsides renews the pathway and fills the scoured channel with another neat, flat layer.

On the hillsides stand cacti swollen from the rain: fat little barrel cacti, multiarmed hedgehog cacti, and the galloping cactus, the cholla, whose living limbs radiate out from a long-dead root stalk. There are trees and shrubs here that have their own methods of desert survival: the creosote bush has varnished leaves to retard evaporation, the *torote* or elephant tree limits its leaves to tiny, evergreen leaflets in complete disproportion to its thigh-sized limbs. Visually dominant on the hillside is the *palo blanco*, perhaps the most beautiful tree in Baja, with its tall, slender, white limbs that reflect heat and its paper-thin leaves that minimize moisture loss. I decide to have lunch in the half-shade of a *palo blanco*: raisins, cheddar cheese, and water.

The best lesson of the arroyo can be gained by sitting in one spot. Within minutes, life activities resume that your exploring had suspended: a grey lizard tongues by, butterflies flit, a Costas humming-bird hovers above my head and then races off on supersonic wings. I hear a breeze work up the arroyo from the sea, carrying the staccato sound of an unseen woodpecker. Not much else moves at noon in heat that is near eighty degrees. The energy of the arroyo lies dormant, to be heard tonight in quick movements and the workings of little jaws.

Our traveling days begin ninety minutes before sunrise, with Charley shaking tents. Like well-oiled machines, we bump and clang in the darkness, filling dry bags and lugging them boatward in an attempt to beat the sun. Periodically, one of us stops to feel for the wind—alert to the first breath that may mean a wind delay. But as the light of the sun turns the Sea of Cortez a brilliant orange, we slide our kayaks into the still water, adjust our paddles, and take the first strokes into a calm day.

Our third travel day, we stay in a loose formation throughout the morning, paddling through the rising heat. On our left, the Gulf of California plays host to passing porpoises and flights of pelicans, and the shore reveals the volcanic layering of red lava and white ash.

Our water supply has dwindled and water sources along the way are few. We take advantage of a passing sloop, manned by winter refugees from Vancouver, British Columbia, who gladly top off our jugs.

There are few travelers along this coast. Offshore, sailboats sometimes mark the horizon, as do the rusty shrimpers and the occasional power yacht. Due to the prevailing north wind, all the kayakers paddle south. There must be at least ten guide services joining NOLS on this route, shepherding groups of kayakers, others at times sharing our bay without crowding. This year there are more people than in years past, but a shared environmental responsibility continues to maintain this coast's wild character.

By noon, we pass Junkyard Beach, our eventual take-out and end of trip. This somber note dwells in our minds, as our arms automatically carve the paddles through the water. A flight of pelicans glides by downwind, inches off the sea's surface. One by one, we notice and follow their movements with fascination.

On the Baja sojourn, the brown pelican is our constant and ever-entertaining neighbor. These large seabirds travel low on the water, drafting the bird ahead—beak to tail feather. They contour the flat swell much as land birds do a thermal, timing short bursts of wing thrusts in relation to the rise of the wave. They gain four to six feet, then glide for all they're worth until their wingtips skim the swell. We watch them go, disappearing around the headland into San Juanico Cove, as much their favorite campsite as ours.

San Juanico is a large, unusually beautiful cove on the southern end of San Basilio Bay. Well protected by high headlands, at its center is a cluster of towering sea stacks crowned by osprey nests. Overhead, magnificent frigatebirds circle, and beyond, in a series of scalloped coves, the pelicans have found a school of *sardinas*. We paddle happily toward the beach, anticipating an extended swim and the simple pleasure of watching the birds.

This is our final camp. Our remaining days are spent snorkeling amidst the diving pelicans, feasting on Charley's daily catch, and listening to the osprey's calls piercing the distance. Lying on the beach, I can't help thinking that someday there's going to be a road into this area—a nagging thought on our last afternoon. The osprey calls again, greeting her mate as he glides across the sky. Together we watch his approach, flare, and landing on the nest.

Suddenly at the shoreline, the water is alive with movement—we stare dumbfounded as Charley sprints to the water's edge and begins scooping fish after fish in our direction. Mullet are beaching themselves to avoid a predator. With Charley's added assistance, they fly through the air, crashing into the bushes to become our dinner instead. We retrieve a bounty of quivering sixteen- to twenty-inch-long fish doomed to the cutting board, the garlic, and the limes. While the fish marinates, we settle back, staring out across the tranquil bay.

As this trip to Baja ends, I am amazed that annually we go through the trouble, risking our necks on the roads, and braving Montezuma's revenge, scorpion bites, and the *federales*, just to spend a few quiet days like these. There is an exotic quality to this coast, where life is so different and so precious, that keeps us returning, repeating the same route south of Mulegé, year after year.

Mangrove Mañana

La Manzanilla

THE CONSTANT SOUND is a dry rasping of palm fronds, the thatch roof of a substantial though neglected *palapa* standing in the wind. The intermittent sound is the surf along the beach, zippering from right to left, sometimes coming ashore with so little force it fails to break, like a heart skipping a beat. I stop and listen through the sudden silence until the rhythmic pattern begins again. In time the wave sequence builds to a height somewhere approaching three feet, and the beach rings with the shrill squeals and laughter of tumbling children.

Occasionally I hear another sound, overhead, muted, and at first unidentifiable—a tracery of big, urgent wing beats passing north to south. It is the sound of an anhinga, a giant cormoran-like bird, flying low and fast for the safety of the mangroves. Before I open my eyes the sound is gone, blended into the simple song of a La Manzanilla afternoon.

Our *palapa* is a simple beach structure common along both coasts of Mexico, made of forked tree-limb uprights that support a beam and thatch roof. It is ideal, because it provides shade and is open to the

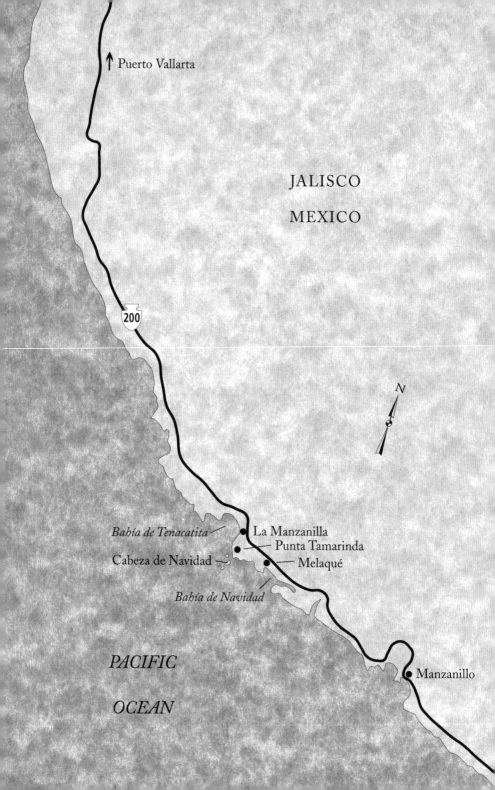

cool breezes of the seashore. Ours is without walls, the only furniture a kitchen table, shelves for supplies, various chairs and campstools, a fence to keep out the animals, and the hammock I now occupy.

A body moves past me. Julie Stimson, the assistant guide, is heading for the beach. Our people must be back—sea kayaking Christmas vacationers bent on what can only be termed relentless fun. I prop myself up in the hammock and watch the approach of the kayaks. Julie wades into the sea, poised with a line to hook on the stern of the first beachbound double in case the kayak begins to broach. The others in singles and doubles wait offshore. One by one the boats come through the surf, legs emerge, dry bags are piled on the beach, and the boats are hiked up past my hammock, past the *palapa*, to be bedded down near our tents.

The people in the group are from Seattle or Anchorage, their once winter-white exteriors now brown in the twenty-degree-latitude sun, their parched interiors intent on the coolers, liquids, fruit juice, and beer.

I suppose I should get up. Soon it will be time for dinner: fresh tamales, a shrimp-and-coconut soup, a dorado fish with a cilantro hot sauce and, with the help of a battery-operated ice crusher, piña coladas. I plant my feet on either side of the hammock and lever up, using reserves of energy saved up over the afternoon. Heading for the tent and a change of clothes to insulate me from the cool of the evening and the dusk assault of mosquitoes, I take a zigzag path to avoid being hit by the head-crushing coconuts that periodically thud into the sand.

La Manzanilla is a town that is not included in the indexes of the Mexico guidebooks, nor does it show up on detailed maps. It is a town on the edge of the Pacific Ocean, two hundred kilometers south of Puerto Vallarta and one hundred kilometers north of Manzanillo. A small road sign along the coastal highway signals its existence, and a dirt road leads from the blacktop three kilometers west to its small grid of dusty streets—home to about six hundred people. They live in small brick and adobe houses, run a few substantial *mercados,* and get baptized, married, and mourned at a new jarringly modern Catholic church. A few families with haciendas on the beach have opened restaurants. But aside from the church and the few new pickup trucks baking in the sun, La Manzanilla has the look of a miniature 1920s banana republic, persisting for generations without much attention from the outside world.

Not that we are the answer to their prayers. Fame, fortune, and tourists may come to La Manzanilla, but not through us. We are incidental visitors, curiosities with kayaks, shopping for food in the *mercado,* buying fish from the *pangas* pulled up on the beach. We are a type the townspeople will probably never see again when and if the long white beach fills in with hotels, golf courses, and T-shirt stands.

Scott Roberge, head guide of Seattle-based Outback Expeditions, wants to know my opinion of the decision to come to La Manzanilla. He's got the question all kayak outfitters ask themselves: Is it a successful idea? This is Outback's first group to visit La Manzanilla after two years of waiting for Mexican licensing and bureaucrats, promotion, and logistics. I reply that it's perfect, in an unusual, on-the-edge-of-wilderness way.

∿∿

Nine days ago we arrived at Puerto Vallarta, one of Mexico's many "gold coasts." Scott collected us from our afternoon flights, and we piled into a van and headed south past the gigantic tourist hotels, the old town, and the slums. I retreated to the back of the van, and from my prone position atop a ton of gear bags I listened to snatches of get-acquainted conversation, as my inverted view changed from highrises and telephone wires to a canopy of second-growth jungle and starlight.

By the time we arrived at base camp we had placed names with faces, hometowns, and professions: an architect, a federal office worker, a teacher, a clothes designer for Eddie Bauer, a stockbroker, and my friend Sarah, a Ph.D. candidate in nursing ethics. We sorted out our bags, and using flashlights found our tents. Paul, the Anchorage stockbroker, suggested a night swim, and the unpacking became a search for bathing suits. Out of the shadows we came, laughing into the surf.

The water was warmer than the night. Waves approached in the darkness, catching us by surprise, breaking with a phosphorescent glow. Along the shore, few signs of man rimmed the bay, called Bahía Tenacatita. Just two clusters of light, an RV enclave and a hotel complex, defined the northern curve. Above them, the North Star and the Great Bear were low on the hills. To the south, the town slumbered under a few incongruously bright mercury vapor lights.

Dawn revealed a dry, tropical landscape of volcanic hills beneath grey-green vegetation. Outcrops of rock punctuated the coast. A few rugged islands known as "the Churches" lay near the mouth of the crescent-shaped bay, and a mangrove swamp nestled behind us, penetrating inland.

For a few days, we acclimatized to the hot, breezy, humid world of the beach and the random events of a town swelling with the arrival of local Guadalajara Christmas vacationers. We learned about kayaks, paddling techniques, beach landings, and self-rescue—each day paddling across Bahía Tenacatita. Taking snorkles and a sun tarp, we visited remote palm-fringed beaches, read and talked, spread corn tortillas with ripe avocados, white fish, and hot sauce, and cooled off with Mexican beer and triple-sweet Mexican soda pop. We relaxed and warmed to an exotic land on the edge of the Pacific.

· THE HIDDEN COAST ·

The noise of a motorcycle, one of those nasty three-wheeled off-road vehicles (ORVs) overloaded with three, maybe four small children, interrupts my thoughts as it blasts down the beach. Trash blows past my tent on the fresh afternoon breeze. I rummage through my bag for a fresh shirt, thinking what a tarnished heaven La Manzanilla is—a paradise on the edge of discovery.

The *palapa* has become a hub of special experiences like the hidden facets of an uncut gem. Each venture into the sunlight is totally different, a crossing into other worlds—from little girls in crisp white confirmation dresses who shyly bid us welcome, to an underwater wilderness, clear, colorful, and quiet beneath the sea. Beyond the hammock lie the sweep and the occasional solitude of the four-mile beach. But one unsuspected world, unknown for three days though only two hundred feet from the *palapa*, would prove to be the finest facet of them all. Sarah remembers: "The moment that stands out for me was discovering the swamp, the mangroves, parrots flying overhead . . . coming around that one corner and seeing the white ibis. I've gone past that page in the bird book and seen that bird a thousand times, but never in the wild."

Sarah and I first paddle the mangrove swamp at dawn on the third morning, going in where the mangrove trees jut toward the sea and neatly hide a narrow surge channel. The waxy-green mangrove leaves, a visual and physical barrier from camp, part and we enter into a series of surprisingly large lakes. The foliage of the rounded mangrove trees hangs over the water; there is no visible bank, no high ground, just a continuous wall of vegetation supported by radial fans of mahogany-red roots that disappear into the turbid, coffee-colored water. By guesswork and the recent signs of Scott and his assistants' machetes—they had cleared some of the routes that had grown impassable—we wind our way deeper into the swamp following tunnel-like passages that take us through an environment different from any we have ever seen.

Mangrove swamps are a belittled biome. The rich foliage of the mangrove tree itself makes it look like your basic tree, but a closer inspection reveals that its roots are in water, saline to fresh, in the shallow lagoons that buffer much of the subtropical to tropical coast-lines of the world. These are difficult environments for man, and despite the fact that they provide habitat and sanctuary to numerous species of plant, animal, bird, and fish, mangroves are routinely destroyed with righteous abandon. But this mangrove swamp on the outskirts of La Manzanilla percolates along in good health without much hindrance from the townspeople.

On our first paddle, Sarah and I explore until we end within earshot of the highway. En route we see more exotic birds than either of us has ever seen at any one time, short of in an aviary. Along with the anhinga, we manage to find a solitary black hawk, a snowy egret, great white herons, a little blue heron, numerous green herons, the tasseled black-crowned night heron, and white ibises. Though the *Golden Field Guide to the Birds of North America* says white ibises are not here, they are. We are ecstatic.

That morning we begin a fascination with the mangrove that in time is shared by all in our group. Once Scott has taken the group through, each day at dawn or dusk a couple of kayakers put in on the channel and disappear through the canopy, returning with stories of flocks of jabbering parrots, the rare sight of a cayman (a tropical American crocodilian), and a roost tree filled with white egrets. On our final evening in La Manzanilla, Sarah catches me at the tent and convinces me that we should take a last paddle through the mangrove together. Dinner can wait.

We check with Scott and he agrees to save us a meal. We grab a couple of Wind Dancers and slide them into the skin-temperature water. As our kayaks clear the entry foliage, a pair of black-crowned night herons leap into the sky, while unseen others sidestep deeper into the jungle of limbs and leaves. As we paddle slowly along the edge of the lake, our ears listen for life just within the canopy, as our eyes watch the far mangrove tops for the long necks and tapered bodies of the many fishing birds home from the sea. In the early evening, as the last direct sun hits the far shore, the swamp is noisy with the classic tropical calls of the wild.

We have improved our ability to spot the various birds perched in the dense branches and root structures, and through our repeated paddles into the swamp, we have learned where most of them congregate. We speed up at times, then drift to a crawl as we pass through a constricted section of overhanging vegetation, just to avoid disturbing the cormorants and ibises on their perches. The water is perfectly still, mirror-imaging the bulging crowns of the mangrove trees in the warm light of sunset. I have a 300-mm telephoto lens on my camera and am waiting for a chance opportunity, when we round a bend and flush a great white heron with a seventy-inch wingspan—the largest bird in residence.

The heron flies down the channel, and just as it turns out of sight it begins to flare, a sure sign that it has landed. We gather speed and then drift, ruddering around the corner, our camera and binoculars ready. For the next ten minutes our boats close the sixty feet to the heron, neither Sarah nor I moving a muscle. My camera and lens become heavy but I dare not move. I shoot a few insurance shots at a distance, and the heron jumps at the clicks. I can feel Sarah just behind me, patient while I stalk the photograph. At fifteen feet, we are still moving with the current at about a foot a minute, when the great bird begins to show signs of anxiety. I shoot a set of pictures as it lifts and flies, again within the channel to another waterside perch. Quietly, we backpaddle and make our way in the gathering dusk.

As the day ends, flights of raucous parrots, bright green with red highlights, skim the treetops. Egrets in a white V follow the pattern of lakes highlighted in the afterglow of sunset. Pairs of ibises stare out at us from their haunts—and, once, a roseate spoonbill voicing the end of the day circles and lands at its preferred night roost. Without speaking, we paddle steadily and carefully past them. In a strange truce, few fly as we progress. Our course is set on the site we've come to call "the Christmas tree."

Scott had talked of it from his days of clearing paths into the mangrove. Some of our friends had found it in their evening forays. It is the night tree of the snowy egrets, an aged mangrove, nearly leafless, centered in a side lagoon that opens to the beach and a backdrop of setting sun behind palms. As we approach the opening, we both slow, and looking right, go still. About one hundred feet away is a white tree, our Christmas tree, decked with snowy egrets—so many they brighten the evening, silhouetted against the failing light. We drift past the clearing and the mangrove closes in again. I do not shoot a picture, technically impossible with what I have. Yet we are happy to leave the egrets to their gregarious evening, safe in their accustomed mangrove.

Satisfied with a final glimpse, we tuck our mental images safely away and turn toward the tarnished heaven of La Manzanilla.

AFTERWORD

As SEA KAYAKING grows from the jealously guarded domain of a handful of eccentric individualists to a favored activity among a growing number of enthusiasts, so *The Hidden Coast* falls into place as an inspiration to paddlers and dreamers.

After reading Joel Rogers's book, it becomes clear why recreational sea kayaking took root on the West Coast. The area is ideal paddling country—from the ice-choked Alaska lagoons to the scorched coast of Mexico, complete with dramatic history and a poignant, fragile present. This shore is home to some of the most spectacular wildlife on the planet, including orcas, grey whales, bears, and an abundance of bird species. Joel's book reminds me that although I've lived and paddled here for the past ten years, I needn't look beyond our own shores for exotic and extraordinary kayaking.

The book's most lasting contribution to sea kayaking, apart from the spotlight it plays on this beautiful shore, is its sustained enthusiasm for West Coast kayaking. It fired me up to get out there and visit the places mentioned, even when they were already familiar to me. Yet the book is almost as titillating for what it doesn't say as for what it does. Just swing the spotlight up or down the shore a few miles, and there's another inlet to explore or another wave-swept beach to wander.

When my son Dylan was seven, we flew into Hotspring Island in the Queen Charlotte Islands, then paddled along the shores of Lyell Island with its devastated, clearcut slopes. Dylan literally choked with astonished rage at the sight of the shattered forest. "Who said they could do that?" he asked indignantly.

For me, *The Hidden Coast* holds an implicit warning. Areas that we love to explore by kayak are on the edge of destruction. The beauty, peace,

· AFTERWORD ·

and wild splendor that Joel highlights are often just a chain-saw blade away from the big stumps of Lyell Island. By bringing these places to the attention of all paddlers and by encouraging kayakers to visit them, maybe such places will be saved. To answer Dylan's question, "We said they could do it by saying nothing." It is going to be harder for kayakers to say nothing, now that "the hidden coast" has been revealed.

—John Dowd, founding editor of *Sea Kayaker* magazine and author of *Sea Kayaking*

· NOTES ·

OIL TO ICE: Prince William Sound (pp. 17–28)

The epigraph for this chapter was excerpted from an article in the *Anchorage Daily News* on the oil spill, August 5, 1989.

After decimation of the sea otter population, federal regulation was enacted when the 1911 North Pacific Fur Seal Convention established initial protection for the sea otter, and the sea otters rebounded to approximately 10,000 animals at the time of the 1989 spill. The Anchorage U.S. Fish and Wildlife Service count of otters killed and recovered in the spill is 1,016, per their report dated December 19, 1989, quoted in Art Davidson's *In the Wake of the* Exxon Valdez (San Francisco: Sierra Club Books, 1989), p. 394.

John Muir's 1902 remark on the Chugach Range is from "The Pacific Coast Glaciers," a chapter in his book *The Harriman Alaska Expedition*, Vol. I. (New York: Doubleday, 1902), p. 132.

GOING OUTSIDE: Chichagof Island (pp. 29–41)

The Tlingit, pronounced, roughly, "Clink-it", live throughout Southeast Alaska. They, along with the mainland Haida, are the northernmost indigenous groups of the Pacific Northwest Coast Indians living in Alaska. Hoonah, meaning "place where the north wind doesn't blow," is the only large Tlingit settlement remaining on Chichagof Island.

THE KNIFE'S EDGE: The Queen Charlotte Islands (pp. 43–54)

George F. MacDonald's observation about the Haida world is from his book *Haida Monumental Art: The Villages of the Queen Charlotte Islands* (Vancouver: University of British Columbia Press, 1983), p. 3.

ORCA: Johnstone Strait to Blackfish Sound (pp. 55–66)

Paul Spong's 1974 statement about the orca is from his article "The Whale Show" in a collection of readings, *Mind in the Waters*, assembled by Joan McIntyre, editor (New York: Charles Scribner's Sons, 1974), p. 173.

Hunting of orcas is discussed in Eric Hoyt, *ORCA: A Whale Called Killer* (Ontario: Camden East, 1984), p. 255. A study by U.S. veterinarian Mark Keyes in 1970 on captive orca whales in Puget Sound revealed that twenty-five percent of the whales sampled had bullet wounds.

Skana, the whale Paul Spong studied for so many years, died of an infection at the age of eighteen. A member of the K-23 pod, she was captured in Puget Sound at the age of five. For the rest of her life, she performed in captivity at the aquarium in Vancouver, British Columbia.

Paul Spong's research contributed to the awareness that orcas respond to sound more readily than to visual cues. He discovered this with Skana, and by the mid-1970s, the Johnstone Strait orcas were being entertained and observed listening to rock music, Paul Horn's flute, synthesized recreations, and recordings of the whales' own sounds.

Paul Spong's research has continued for thirty years on Hanson Island, where David Arcese's sea kayaking groups periodically visit. For more information on Spong's research, see Rex Weyler's *Song of the Whale* (Garden City, New York: Doubleday, 1986).

Research into whale sounds is an ongoing area of study. Some research indicates that whales "echolocate" to "see" under water. According to this research, by using rapid high- and low-frequency clicks, an orca can identify fish species, maintain spatial relations with the pod, and avoid obstacles. For additional information on orcas and whales in general, see McIntyre, *Mind in the Waters*.

POINT OF CONTACT: Nootka Sound (pp. 67–76)

The derivation of the name Yuquot is discussed in Hilary Stewart's book *The Adventures and Sufferings of John R. Jewitt, Captive of Maquinna* (Vancouver: Douglas & McIntyre, 1987), p. 14.

SOUTH FORK: The Skagit River Estuary (pp. 77–101)

My "Eternal Thermos" was so named for its opportune arrival at the side of my boat during an outing on the Skagit flood of 1979. A stainless steel, two-quart Thermos, it was unaccountably cast adrift upstream and still had warm coffee—black—in it.

The first wintering of snow geese in the Skagit River estuary is discussed in an unpublished paper by Larry Brewer dated 1976. Brewer was once the Skagit state game range manager, and introduced me to estuaries. He is now an environmental quality manager at the Institute for Wildlife Environmental Toxicology at Clemson University in Clemson, South Carolina.

SHI SHI: The Olympic Peninsula Seashore (pp. 103–111)

Glen Sims's song is titled "Go To Sea Once More." A tune reminiscent of "Greensleeves," it was known as a "forebitter"—a type of sea shanty sung off watch in the forward crew's quarters, or fo'c'sle, of sailing ships. This particular version was popular with the sailors of Liverpool and has no known author or date of origin. For information, see Stan Hugill's *Shanties from the Seven Seas* (New York: E. P. Dutton & Co., 1961), pp. 581–85.

The comment about the development of rogue waves in the ocean is from K. E. Lilly, Jr., *Marine Weather of Western Washington* (Seattle: Starpath Publications, 1983), p. 29.

· NOTES ·

PADDLE TO THE SEA (pp. 127–168)

From May 4, 1804, to September 24, 1806, the Corps of Discovery, twenty-eight men plus Sacajawea and her son (born enroute), forged a nine-thousand-mile journey from St. Louis to the Pacific Ocean and back without loss of life, on a route planned to avoid Spanish claims to the south as well as to make expeditious use of the Missouri and Columbia Rivers. Once gaining the Columbia at the present-day location of the Tri-Cities, 325 miles from the river's mouth, the expedition took twenty-one days to reach the Pacific. After building and wintering over at Fort Clatsop, just west of the present site of Astoria, they returned upriver in May, taking thirty-seven days before bartering their canoes and continuing on foot with pack horses at Arlington on the Oregon side, 102 miles below the Tri-Cities.

The first quotation from William Clark's journal is from *The History of the Expedition under the Command of Lewis and Clark*, edited by Elliott Coues, and originally published in four volumes in 1893. It is a faithful, detailed, well-documented work compared to the earlier published account by Nicolas Biddle, 1814. Most importantly, as the account proceeds, one can locate where the Corps of Discovery was relative to present-day landmarks. The contemporary edition in three volumes was published by Dover Publications, New York. A recent work, *Our Natural History, the Lessons of Lewis and Clark*, 1995, by Daniel B. Botkin is also worth noting, as it attempts to quantify, detail, and compare Lewis and Clark's frontier wilderness with today's.

Of interest regarding the "hot side of the river," the western shore of the Hanford Site, where the nuclear reactors and old nuclear processing grounds are located, there are 11 tons of radioactive plutonium 239 stored and monitored at Hanford and an estimated 1.5 tons in the soils and pipes of the Hanford Site yet to be retrieved. Inhaling just 0.27 micrograms of plutonium, the half-life of which is 24,100 years, can bring about cancer (according to Glenn Zorpette, in "Confronting the Nuclear Legacy, Part II," *Scientific American* 274:5, May 1996, p. 92).

Numbers of salmon and steelhead on the Columbia River of Lewis and Clark's day that I use are a best mid-range estimate. *Our Natural History, the Lessons of Lewis and Clark*, by Daniel B. Botkin, gives a reasoned assessment as well as catch figures through the heyday of the salmon canneries on the river.

One of the most timely and informative overviews of the history and current issues on the Columbia and Snake Rivers can be found in Blaine Harden's *A River Lost: The Life and Death of the Columbia*, 1996. Another good writer and a source with a similar intent is William Dietrich's *Northwest Passage: The Great Columbia River*, 1996.

The scientific name for the sea otter, *Enhydris marina*, was provided by William

· NOTES ·

Clark in one of his journal quotes. (Today the scientific name for the species is *Enhydra lutris*.) Lewis and Clark cite the sea otter as far upriver as the Clark Fork in Idaho. In the natural history description of the species, Clark clearly differentiates between the sea otter and the common, or river otter (*Our Natural History: the Lessons of Louis and Clark*, pp. 852–3). Scientists in recent decades have stated that, "Certainly the great numbers of sea otters in the Columbia River, as far up as Celilo Falls, recorded by Lewis and Clark, were not sea otters but harbor seals, *Foca vigilina* ." See Karl W. Kenyon, *The Sea Otter in the Eastern Pacific Ocean* (New York: Dover Publications, 1975), p. 185.

The buoy I encountered at the mouth of the Columbia is the navigation buoy "QG 7 bell." The "Q" stands for "quick flashing light"; the "G" stands for "green," to inform mariners this is the starboard side of the outgoing channel; the "7" indicates the buoy's location and identifying number; "bell" signifies the sound the buoy makes.

GUNKHOLING: The Oregon and California Coasts (pp. 169–180)

A fine regional book that delves into the history of the area's backroads is Mike Hayden's *Exploring the North Coast* (San Francisco: Chronicle Books, 1982).

The *Coast Pilot* is a fascinating and invaluable source of coastal marine information, tables, charts, and photographs published by the U.S. Government to supplement the nautical charts. See *The United States Coast Pilot*, Vol. 7, *Pacific Coast: California, Oregon, Washington, and Hawaii*, 25th ed. (Washington, D.C.: National Ocean Service, 1989), p. 201.

ANACAPA CROSSING: The Santa Barbara Channel Islands (pp. 181–191)

A comprehensive source of information on Anacapa Island and the other channel islands is Karen Jones Dowty's *A Visitor's Guide: The California Channel Islands* (Ventura, California: Seaquit Books, 1984).

The comment made about the enthusiasm of early Aleut sea otter hunters is from Adele Ogden, *The California Sea Otter Trade 1784–1848*, Vol. 26, (Berkeley: University of California Publications, 1941), p. 13. This book offers the most detailed description of the sea otter trade of that time.

Data on sea otter harvests in the nineteenth century are from George B. Dyson, "An Illicit Alliance—the California Sea Otter Boom of 1803–1841," *Sea Kayaker* 4:1, Summer 1987, p. 11. This article, as well as George Dyson's book *Baidarka* (Seattle: Alaska Northwest Books, 1986), provide an in-depth look at the Aleuts and their sea kayaks and a historical account of their involvement in the California sea otter hunt. Another detailed account of the Aleuts can be found in the translation of Ivan Veniaminov's 1840 *Notes on the Islands of the Unalaska District*, translated by Lydia Black and R. H. Geoghegan and edited by

· NOTES ·

Richard A. Pierce (Fairbanks: Limestone Press, University of Alaska History Department, 1984). Richard Batman's *The Outer Coast* (New York: Harcourt Brace Jovanovich, 1985) provides a good overview of the West Coast of North America through the era.

THE TRANSLUCENT SEA: Baja and the Sea of Cortez (pp. 193–202)

The epigraphs for this chapter are from Johann Jakob Baeger, S.J., *Observations in Lower California*, 1772, translated by M. M. Brandenburg and Carl L. Baumann (Berkeley: University of California Press, 1952), p. 5; and Octavio Paz, "The Broken Jar," *The Selected Poems of Octavio Paz, translated by Muriel Rukeyser* (Bloomington: Indiana University Press, 1968), p. 165.

John Steinbeck's quote is from *Log from the Sea of Cortez* (New York: Penguin Books, 1986, p. 54.

Joseph Wood Krutch, *Baja California and the Geography of Hope* (San Francisco: Sierra Club Books, 1967), p. 34.

· ACCESS GUIDE ·

A NOTE ON SAFETY AND ACCESS: The information in *The Hidden Coast* is not intended to provide instruction on safely paddling or leading any of the trips. For educational information, see books like John Dowd's *Sea Kayaking*. The listing below for degree of difficulty—beginner, intermediate, and expert—indicates a varied marine environment from safe to dangerous in average weather conditions.

OIL TO ICE: Prince William Sound, Alaska (pp. 17–28)

LOCATION: 50 miles east-southeast of Anchorage, Alaska. Due west of Cordova.

SEASON: From May 15 to September 15. Best May 15 to June 1, for the fewest bugs and best bird-watching; July for best summer weather.

TRIP LENGTH: Prince William Sound calls for extended stays. From Whittier, it takes 1 week minimum to paddle to Harriman Fjord and back; 2 weeks is optimal for that area. Consider a shuttle to get you to Knight Island.

DEGREE OF DIFFICULTY: Beginner (with expert companions) to expert.

GETTING THERE/PUT-IN: By air to Anchorage. Charter air service on floats for remote drop-off by Ketchum Air, tel. (800) 433-9114. To Whittier put-in, take Alaska Direct Busline, tel. (800) 780-6652 for 50-mile trip to Portage, where the Alaska Railroad, tel. (800) 544-0552 provides 6 daily trains to Whittier from May 15 to September 15 and 3 shuttles a week during the remainder of the year. Cordova has daily jet service to southeast Prince William Sound.

PUT-IN: Whittier public boat launch.

INFORMATION: Alaska State Tourism Bureau, P.O. Box E, Juneau, Alaska 99811, tel. (907) 465-2010, www.dced.state.ak.us/tourism.

RESERVATIONS/ACCOMMODATIONS: Hotels at both Whittier (rustic) and Cordova. Reservations advised.

GUIDES/RENTALS/SHUTTLES: For information on guides, kayak rentals, and boat shuttles contact the City of Whittier Visitors Center, Box 608, Whittier, Alaska 99693, tel. (907) 472-2327, fax: 472-2404.

CAUTIONS: Glacier winds, glacier icefall waves, icebergs, high tides, bears, rain, oil tankers and other ships.

LOGISTICS: Kelley Weaverling publishes a kayaker's map of Prince William Sound showing a selected number of routes and campsites with handy information on the back. Available for $7.95 from Orca Books, P.O. Box 1308, Cordova, Alaska, tel. (907) 424-5305. The chart for western Prince William Sound is NOAA chart 16700.

GOING OUTSIDE: Chichagof Island, Alaska (pp. 29–41)

LOCATION: 75 miles west of Juneau, Alaska.

SEASON: May through August; best June and July.

TRIP LENGTH: At least 9 days. July is usually the best month for clear days.

· ACCESS GUIDE ·

DEGREE OF DIFFICULTY: Intermediate with expert accompaniment.

GETTING THERE: By air to Juneau or Sitka. Alaska ferry from Bellingham, Washington, or Prince Rupert, British Columbia, will take hard-shell kayaks to Sitka, Juneau, Hoonah, or Pelican: Alaska Marine Highway System, 1591 Glacier Avenue, Juneau, Alaska 99801-1427, tel. (800) 642-0066. www.state.ak.us ("hot topics"). Charter floatplane: Alaska Seaplane Service, tel. (800) 478-3360.

PUT-IN: Pelican is the closest northern put-in; Sitka is the southern put-in.

INFORMATION: Alaska State Tourism Bureau, P.O. Box E, Juneau, Alaska 99811, tel. (907) 465-2010, www.dced.state.ak.us/tourism.

RESERVATIONS/ACCOMMODATIONS: The U.S. Forest Service cabin at White Sulphur Hot Springs should be reserved months in advance. Contact Tongass National Forest, tel. (907) 747-6671, www.fs.fed.us/r10/tongass.

GUIDE SERVICE: Spirit Walker Expeditions, P.O. Box 240, Gustavus, Alaska 99826, tel. (907) 697-2266, www.hw.net/~kayak.

CAUTIONS: Open ocean coast with frequent storms, rainfall, and fog. Bears on main island.

LOGISTICS: The Alaska ferries make this one of the most easily accessed wilderness traveling destinations for hard-shell kayaks. See NOAA charts 17322 and 17321.

THE KNIFE'S EDGE: The Queen Charlotte Islands, B.C. (pp. 43–54)

LOCATION: 80 miles west of Prince Rupert, British Columbia; 350 miles from Vancouver, British Columbia.

SEASON: May through September 15; best in May for wildlife.

TRIP LENGTH: 2 weeks one way, 3 to 4 weeks for a round-trip.

DEGREE OF DIFFICULTY: Intermediate.

GETTING THERE: By air from Vancouver, B.C., to Sandspit in the Queen Charlotte Islands. By water, take the B.C. Ferries from Port Hardy on the north end of Vancouver Island and/or from Prince Rupert to Queen Charlotte City; tel. (604) 386-3431, www.bcferries.com. Air Charter: Trans-Provincial Aviation, tel. (604) 637-5355. Float plane charters out of Queen Charlotte City: South Moresby Air Charters, tel. (250) 559-4222. Out of Sandspit: Harbour Air, tel. (250) 627-1341.

PUT-IN: Kayakers can put in from a dock adjacent to the ferry landing at Queen Charlotte City, or find a car shuttle to Moresby Camp via the interisland ferry, 25 miles south, or hire a boat or plane shuttle.

INFORMATION/RESERVATIONS: The South Moresby area is now called Gwaii Haanas. For general information on access and reservations, contact The British Columbia Office of Tourism: (800) HELLOBC [(800) 435-5622]. To visit Gwaii

Haanas you must secure a reservation, pay a fee per person per day, and visit the Parks Canada/Haida Gwaii office in Queen Charlotte City for an orientation before traveling south. Tel. (250) 559-8818.

GUIDES: Parks Canada in Queen Charlotte City has a list of approved guides. Tel. (250) 559-8818.

CAUTIONS: Sudden northwest winds off the crest of South Moresby Island can rip through the inlets on the east side. Caution is advised when making the open crossing to Ninstints.

LOGISTICS: If you are going without a guide, the best trip is the three-week experience following our route starting southbound. For shorter routes, consider breakdowns and paddling south with a floatplane pickup ($$$). The great trip would be a circumpaddle of Gwaii Haanas (South Moresby)—experts only.

ORCA: Johnstone Strait, B.C. (pp. 55–66)

LOCATION: On the north side of Vancouver Island, British Columbia, 150 miles northwest of Vancouver, B.C., and 295 miles from Seattle.

SEASON: Mid-June through October; best July through September.

TRIP LENGTH: Allow 6 days for viewing the whales and the territory.

DEGREE OF DIFFICULTY: Beginner to advanced. Leaders should be familiar with strong tides and standing waves.

GETTING THERE: By car from Vancouver, take the B.C. ferry from either Tsawwassen or Horseshoe Bay to Nanaimo, Vancouver Island, and go north on Highway 19 to Port McNeill. Flights from Vancouver International Airport to Port Hardy: Pacific Coastal Airlines, tel. (800) 663-2872. Out of Seattle, Sound Flight, tel. (800) 825-0722, or Kenmore Air, tel. (800) 424-5526, to Port McNeill. Taxi to Telegraph Cove.

PUT-IN: Telegraph Cove for parking and launching, with fees rising. Lots of new development has changed the feeling of this place, since.

ACCOMMODATIONS: Port McNeill has several hotels and motels that tend to be crowded during the summer. There is a campground at Telegraph Cove.

INFORMATION AND RESERVATIONS: British Columbia Office of Tourism, tel. (800) 663-6000. Port McNeill Tourist Information and Reservations, tel. (604) 956-3131.

GUIDES: Northern Lights Expeditions paddles Johnstone Strait from June into September. Contact them at P.O. Box 4289, Bellingham, WA 98227, tel. (800) 754-7402, (360) 734-6334; www.seakayaking.com.

CAUTIONS: Blackney Pass and Weynton Passage have tidal currents in excess of 10 knots. Use the Canadian current tables and pass through at slack. Johnstone is a wind tunnel with particularly active storms from the southeast. At all times, watch out for ships when crossing major channels. Camping in Robson Bight is against the law. There are a few campsites along the Vancouver Island shore midway between the bight and Telegraph Cove. They can be very crowded in the summer—plan trips for early or late summer. Stay in this area briefly, and plan to tour the rest of the region, which has more campsite options. Noseeums, the diminutive stinging insects, haunt most camps, especially along the Vancouver side of Johnstone Strait.

LOGISTICS: Keep a plastic bag handy in case a friendly fisherman offers a salmon. The B.C. ferries leave on time, and there can be a wait on Friday afternoons. See CHS chart 3456.

POINT OF CONTACT: Nootka Sound, Vancouver Island, B.C. (pp. 67–76)

LOCATION: At the midpoint of Vancouver Island's west coast, 150 miles northwest of Vancouver, B.C.

SEASON: May through September; best in August through September.

TRIP LENGTH: 4 days.

DEGREE OF DIFFICULTY: Beginner to expert.

GETTING THERE: From Vancouver by car, take the B.C. ferry from either Tsawwassen or Horseshoe Bay to Nanaimo. Drive north on Highway 19 up the east coast of Vancouver Island to Campbell River, then west on Highway 28 through Gold River to the dock on Muchalat Inlet. The *Uchuck III* departs at 8 A.M. unless otherwise stated every day except Sun, Mon, from July 1 through September 15. The rest of the year the boat departs every Tues, Thurs, and Fri. Call for reservations, tel. (250) 283-2515, www.island.net\~mvuchuck\.

INFORMATION: British Columbia Office of Tourism, tel. (800) 663-6000; B.C. ferry information, tel. (250) 386-3431.

ACCOMMODATIONS: Gold River has motels, and a good campground is located on the highway midway between the town and the dock.

CAUTIONS: There are numerous reefs along the outer coast north of Friendly Cove.

LOGISTICS: Expect a 5- to 6-hour drive from Nanaimo to Gold River. It would be good to have a handheld VHF radio if you intend to return on the *Uchuck III* and need to make contact; contact can be made through the lighthouse crew at Friendly Cove as well. The food and crew aboard the *Uchuck III* are excellent. See CHS chart 3664.

SOUTH FORK: The Skagit River Estuary, Washington (pp. 77–101)

LOCATION: 60 miles north of Seattle, 88 miles south of Vancouver, B.C.

SEASON: Year-round; best in mid-May, September.

TRIP LENGTH: Day trip.

DEGREE OF DIFFICULTY: Beginner.

GETTING THERE/PUT-IN: From Highway I-5, take the Starbird exit 218, which is

1 mile south of Conway, go west to the road's end, and cross the railroad tracks. There's parking along the river road past the boat launch.

INFORMATION: For hunting season dates, contact State Fish and Wildlife Information, tel. (360) 902-2200.

ACCOMMODATIONS: Lodging is available at numerous bed-and-breakfast establishments and motels in the area. Call Northwest Washington Tourism for information, tel. (206) 221-TOUR.

GUIDES/RENTALS: Northwest Outdoor Center, 2100 Westlake Ave. North, Seattle, Washington 98109, tel. (206) 281-9694.

CAUTIONS: Make sure the outgoing tide does not leave you stranded on the tideflats. Take care to note the characteristics of the slough you have paddled as you enter the bay, if you intend to return the same way you came. Avoid the estuary during spring and winter floods when flood warnings are in effect.

LOGISTICS: Bring a bird book, binoculars, camera, and drinking water. Plan to stop at an isolated cedar stump to "blind-up" for lunch and watch the natural activities. Bring knee-high boots; in summer, try going barefoot. See topographic maps for La Conner and Utsalady.

SHI SHI: The Olympic Peninsula Seashore, Washington (pp. 103–111)

LOCATION: Northwest corner of Washington state's Olympic Peninsula, 150 miles from Seattle.

SEASON: Year-round. Best in the summer, for clear days and almost-warm water.

TRIP LENGTH: At least 3 days.

DEGREE OF DIFFICULTY: Expert. In summer, intermediates with surf-experienced experts.

GETTING THERE/PUT-IN: From the Seattle area, take the Washington state ferry from Seattle to Bainbridge Island or from Edmonds to Kingston, tel. (800) 464-6400, www.wsdot.wa.gov/ferries. Take Highway 305 or 104, respectively, to join Highway 101 north past Port Angeles. Then take Highway 112 north to Neah Bay. Follow the main road west through town, and go south following the Air Force Base signs for 2 miles. Cross the Waatch River bridge, heading south, and stay right. Makah Bay is 1.5 miles from the bridge, the first good put-in. The second put-in is 1.7 miles beyond the first; stay right, cross the Sooes River, and go to the long beach. Watch for the last beach access before the hill. Travel time: 2 1/2 to 3 hours driving plus a 40-minute ferry crossing. There are long ferry waits on summer weekends. Trailer traffic is heavy on Highway 101.

INFORMATION: Olympic National Park, tel. (360) 452-4501.

GUIDES/RENTALS: Northwest Outdoor Center teaches surf skills at Makah Bay every summer: 2100 Westlake Ave. North, Seattle, Washington 98109, tel. (206) 281-9694.

· ACCESS GUIDE ·

CAUTIONS: In winter, high tides and rough seas can make beach landings impossible. Surf is higher on the northern end of Shi Shi Beach. Take great care around the arches. Fog is frequent in the summer. Bring a tide book and carry a VHF radio or good weather radio for weather reports.

LOGISTICS: Due to car vandalism, it's advisable to leave little gear in the car. The last house at the top of the hill past the second put-in will take care of your car for a nominal fee per day. In winter, be prepared for rain—bring extra tarps and knee-high boots. There are good campsites in the trees along the beach margin past Petroleum Creek. Carry your water in, or purify water from Petroleum Creek. See topographic maps for Cape Flattery, Makah Bay, and Ozette.

EMBAYMENTS: Willapa, Coos, and San Francisco Bays (pp. 113–125)

Willapa Bay, Washington

LOCATION: Washington state, 124 miles southwest of Seattle.

TRIP LENGTH: Day trip.

DEGREE OF DIFFICULTY: Beginner.

GETTING THERE/PUT-IN: By car from Seattle, go south on Highway I-5 to Highway 101, west to Highway 12, west to Highway 107, south to Highway 101, and south past South Bend to Willapa Bay. Look for put-ins near the highway.

INFORMATION: The Pacific County Museum in South Bend can provide information about the region, tel. (360) 875-5224.

ACCOMMODATIONS: Contact the River Cities Chamber of Commerce, tel. (360) 423-8400.

GUIDES: None. Note that local paddlers with the cooperation of the Washington Watertrails Association have built an overnight and day-use human-powered-watercraft-only Willapa Bay Watertrail. Contact the Washington Watertrails Association, for membership, information, and volunteering, at 4649 Sunnyside Ave. N., Room 305, Seattle, Washington 98103-6900, tel. (206) 545-9161, www.wwta.org.

CAUTIONS: The mud, and getting stranded by the outgoing tide.

LOGISTICS: The quieter you are on this trip the more you'll see. Bring knee-high boots, and a big bag for muddied things on return. See NOAA chart 18504.

Coos Bay, Oregon

LOCATION: Oregon, on the southcentral coast, 215 miles southwest of Portland, 510 miles north of San Francisco.

SEASON: Year-round to Charleston, May through August is best including going outside to Sunset Bay.

TRIP LENGTH: Day trip to 3 days.

DEGREE OF DIFFICULTY: Beginner.

GETTING THERE: Coos Bay can be accessed along the Oregon coast by Highway 101. Driving south on I-5, take Highway 38 to Reedsport and go south to Coos Bay. Driving north, take Highway 42 to Coos Bay.

PUT-IN: The Coos River has few put-ins or take-outs and its banks are muddy. For the South Fork access, follow Highway 101 south through Coos Bay to Bunker Hill, going left to Eastside over the bridge and left through Eastside following the arterial. Cross Catching Slough going east and follow the Coos River along its south bank, following signs to Dellwood. Watch for the county boat launch signs roughly 10 miles from Eastside. Shuttle by cab is inexpensive. The best take-outs are just past the Highway 101 bridge on the south bank, at the public boat launch on the northeast end of the Coos Bay airport runway. This take-out is without a phone; having a VHF radio would allow you to call the marine operator on Channel 25 for a taxi. Charleston harbor boat launch has all the amenities. If you go out the bar, south around Cape Arago is Sunset Beach, a safe surf landing, with a pay phone at the park camping area entrance.

INFORMATION: Oregon State Tourism Bureau, tel. (800) 547-7842, www.travel oregon.com.

ACCOMMODATIONS: There are numerous inexpensive motels and an excellent state park system. Sunset Bay State Park west of Charleston is one of the best paddling parks on the coast.

CAUTIONS: Avoid the river during periods of heavy rainfall in winter and spring. Bar conditions are at their worst during afternoon ebb tides. Stay clear of big ships under way in the channel.

LOGISTICS: The Coos Bay Pilot's Association Tide Tables, P.O. Box 2543, Coos Bay, Oregon 97420, tel. (541) 267-6555, are invaluable sources of maritime information as well as taxis, weather, and bar condition, tel. (541) 888-3102. See NOAA chart 18578.

San Francisco Bay, California

LOCATION: San Francisco Bay, from the Marin Peninsula to San Francisco's Aquatic Park.

SEASON: Year-round.

TRIP LENGTH: Day trip.

DEGREE OF DIFFICULTY: Intermediate to expert, depending on wind and tide conditions.

GETTING THERE/PUT-IN: From San Francisco, take the Golden Gate Bridge going north. Take the Sausalito exit to Fort Baker, and find the small harbor at the base of the bridge's north pylon.

INFORMATION/RESERVATIONS/ACCOMMODATIONS: California State Tourism Department, tel. (800) 862-2543, www.gocalif.ca.gov.

225

GUIDES/RENTALS: Sea Trek, 85 Liberty Ship Way, Sausalito, Schoonmaker Marina, California 94965, tel. (415) 332-4457, www.seatrekkayak.com.

CAUTIONS: Around the bridge, there are strong wind gusts, tides, and eddylines. Strong afternoon winds combined with an outgoing tide can be risky. Heavy ship and boat traffic.

LOGISTICS: There are sea lions around Fisherman's Wharf. Ask for your latté in a cup instead of a glass. See NOAA chart 18649.

PADDLE TO THE SEA: The Columbia River (pp. 127–168)

Hanford Reach to McNary Dam

LOCATION: The Hanford Reach of the Columbia River is in southeastern Washington state between the Priest Rapids Dam, river mile 396 (upstream), and the northern outskirts of Richland (Tri-Cities) at river mile 345. From there the Columbia passes into the McNary Pool, which ends at the McNary Dam at river mile 293 near the Oregon town of Umatilla.

SEASON: Year-round.

TRIP LENGTH: The trip from Vernita Bar through the McNary Pool to Umatilla and the McNary Dam (river mile 293) is 93 miles.

DEGREE OF DIFFICULTY: Intermediate, beginners okay with more experienced paddlers.

GETTING THERE/PUT-IN: By car, the Hanford Reach is accessed at the upstream point on the north side of the Columbia at Vernita Bar, approximately 1 mile above the Vernita Bridge at river mile 388. If you choose to day trip the Reach, there is a take-out on the east side of the river approximately 18 miles downstream at the White Bluffs boat launch, $1/2$ mile southwest of the Grant County/Franklin County boundary (access highway 24 from the north) and 37 miles downstream at the Ringold Hatchery (access from either north or south from Tri-Cities). If you intend to camp on the Reach, check with the phone number below for a proposed camp site at the White Bluffs Landing. You need a map as detailed as the *Washington Atlas and Gazetteer* by DeLorme but not four-wheel drive to negotiate these dirt roads.

INFORMATION/RESERVATIONS/ACCOMMODATIONS: The U.S. Fish and Wildlife Service is currently the keeper of the Hanford Reach. You are free to paddle through the Hanford Site but you cannot land on either side of the river except for the specific boat launches as noted, unless you obtain permission from the Project Leader of the Arid Lands Complex, tel. (509) 371-1801

GUIDES: None.

CAUTIONS: Recent discoveries of radioactive seepage near the old reactors are a caution. Best to keep to the more interesting left side of the Columbia. Current is something to be careful about but there are no rapids. Wind is an issue anywhere on the Columbia, but on this reach worst below Tri-Cities. Also, with the confluence of the Snake River you are paddling a navigable waterway, so watch for both tugs and barges as well as pleasure craft. Note as well that there are jet-boats on the Reach moving at high speeds. The river will rise without warning.

LOGISTICS: Bring water, a bird guide, and a star book for sure. If you obtain permission to camp on the Reach or anywhere south, refrain from making fires, as wood is scarce and most wood is usually a home for some creature. Best to rely on topographic maps for the Hanford Reach. Charts are available as are books of charts for the remaining downstream river. I used the *River Cruising Atlas: Columbia, Snake, Willamette,* published by Evergreen Pacific Publishing.

Portland to the Pacific

LOCATION: From 16 river miles up the Willamette through Portland, Oregon, to the Columbia, north then west to Astoria and the Pacific Ocean.

SEASON: Year-round.

TRIP LENGTH: 108 miles.

DEGREE OF DIFFICULTY: Beginner to intermediate, with the exception of the mouth of the Columbia River. See Cautions below.

GETTING THERE/PUT-IN: I chose to put in at Willamette Park on the south bank of the Willamette off Macadam Avenue. Suburban parking. If you shuttle, plan for a two-hour one-way shuttle to Ilwaco, a good take-out roughly one mile upriver from Cape Disappointment. There is shuttle parking at Ilwaco at the marina. Check at the Port of Ilwaco, Port Captain's Office, for fees.

INFORMATION/RESERVATIONS/ACCOMMODATIONS: Motels and Bed & Breakfasts in all reasonably sized towns. Skamokawa Town Center, 1391 W. State Route 4, Skamokawa, Washington 98647, tel. (360) 795-8300, 1 (888) 920-2777, www.skamokawapaddle.com. Skamokawa Inn B & B is part of the Skamokawa Center, located in a fully restored historic building with nine rooms, each with a view. On the first floor is a restaurant (breakfast and lunch only), a post office, and general store with a good wine selection.

GUIDES: Skamokawa Town Center rents canoes and kayaks provides charts, and makes recommendations on where to paddle. They offer also kayak tours of exploration and discovery, kayak and canoe rentals, clinics, and custom tours. Note that local paddlers with the cooperation of the Washington Watertrails Association are roughing out a human-powered-watercraft-only Lewis and Clark Watertrail on the Columbia. Their first effort and campsites are in this section. Contact the Washington Watertrails Association for information and volunteering at 4649 Sunnyside Ave. N., Room 305, Seattle, Washington 98103-6900, tel. (206) 545-9161, www.wwta.org.

CAUTIONS: I do not recommend that you paddle the bar of the Columbia. It is a subtle bottleneck where the currents can reach seven to eight knots—fast enough to run a buoy underwater. In my conversations with the bar pilots who conn all shipping in and out of this one point, I've learned that the danger begins not just below Astoria but below Tongue Point four miles upriver from town. So if you paddle south of this point I suggest you stick to the Washington side, know the tide cycle, read the depths from a good chart to follow where the volume is going, and watch out for those groins—do not consider running through a gap in a groin because you may get entrapped. Note also that the current tables are known by the pilots as "book time," not necessarily the actual time of the current change because of the fluctuating discharge of the river. Listed times may be off by as much as an hour. Finally, offshore there are a northward-setting current and ever-changing shallows as well as increasing winds and rising swells. Be more than careful, and consider taking out at Ilwaco.

LOGISTICS: Carry a one- to two-day supply of water. Charts are available, as are books of charts, for the remaining downstream river. I used the *River Cruising Atlas: Columbia, Snake, Willamette,* published by Evergreen Pacific Publishing.

GUNKHOLING: The Oregon and California Coasts (pp. 169–180)

The Lost Coast, Northern California

LOCATION: Northern California, 50 miles south of Eureka. From Seattle, 630 miles; from San Francisco, 325 miles.

SEASON: May to August.

TRIP LENGTH: 27 miles from Mattole Beach to Shelter Cove, 1 to 2 days.

DEGREE OF DIFFICULTY: Expert.

GETTING THERE/PUT-IN: Take Highway 101 to Highway 1, and go through Ferndale, south to Petrolia, then west to the Mattole River mouth.

INFORMATION/RESERVATIONS/ACCOMMODATIONS: County park camping.

CAUTIONS: Expect wind, strong currents, and fog. Drivers use low gear on downgrade into Shelter Cove.

LOGISTICS: Water available. Shuttle time from Shelter Cove to Mattole River one way: 3 hours.

Heceta Head, Oregon

LOCATION: Midpoint on the Oregon Coast, 181 miles southwest of Portland, 171 miles north of the California/Oregon border.

SEASON: May through September.

TRIP LENGTH: Day trip.

DEGREE OF DIFFICULTY: Intermediate to expert, depending on the weather and surf.

GETTING THERE/PUT-IN: Highway 101 to Devil's Elbow State Park.

INFORMATION/RESERVATIONS/ACCOMMODATIONS: Oregon State Tourism Department, tel. (800) 547-7842.

CAUTIONS: Do not enter the Sea Lion Caves. The ocean conditions are active.

LOGISTICS: The park closes at sunset.

Cape Meares, Oregon

LOCATION: Northern Oregon Coast, 80 miles west of Portland.

SEASON: May through September.

TRIP LENGTH: Day trip.

DEGREE OF DIFFICULTY: Intermediate to expert, depending on sea conditions.

GETTING THERE/PUT-IN: Highway 101, or from Portland via Highway 8 to Tillamook. Follow the signs to Oceanside, and put in at the town beach.

INFORMATION/RESERVATIONS/ACCOMMODATIONS: Oregon State Tourism Department, tel. (800) 547-7842. The closest campsite is at Cape Lookout State Park below Netarts.

CAUTIONS: Open ocean conditions.

LOGISTICS: The offshore rocks are a sensitive environmental area and a National Wildlife Refuge—no trespassing. The extensive beaches of the Tillamook bar may be accessed for hiking from the Cape Meares loop road. See NOAA chart 18558.

ANACAPA CROSSING: The Santa Barbara Channel Islands, California (pp. 181–191)

LOCATION: The Santa Barbara area of Southern California, 60 miles northwest of Los Angeles.

SEASON: Year-round. March is known for strong winds and great wildflowers. There's the least wind in late summer, with the best conditions in September.

TRIP LENGTH: 26 miles to and from Anacapa Island. Minimum 3 days, 4 days would be excellent. There is a strong possibility of being stranded on the island due to high winds.

DEGREE OF DIFFICULTY: Expert.

GETTING THERE/PUT-IN: Highway 101 to Oxnard. Head west to Victoria Avenue, take a left, and head south along the east side of Channel Islands Harbor to a park locally known as Hobie Beach just south of the Coast Guard Station.

INFORMATION/RESERVATIONS/ACCOMMODATIONS: California Tourism Department, tel. (800) 862-2543, www.gocalif.ca.gov. For kayaker's information contact California Kayak Friends, 14252 Culver Drive, A-199, Tustin, California 92604, www.ckf.org. For required Anacapa and Santa Rosa Islands camping reservations, contact Channel Islands National Park headquarters, 1901 Spinnaker Drive, Ventura Harbor, California 93001-4354, tel. (805) 658-5700, www.channel.islands.national-park.com. Although there are limited campsites, there are frequent last-minute cancellations.

GUIDES: Southwind Kayak Center, 17855 Skypark Circle #A, Irvine, CA 92614, tel. (800) 768-8494, (949) 261-0200, www.southwindkayaks.com.

CAUTIONS: Be prepared for fog, northwest winds, short and steep seas, and ship traffic. The current, nicknamed the "rotary," can reach a speed of 2 knots and is unpredictable. High-speed recreational boaters use the same course as kayakers. Visually check for landmarks on the outbound leg, to aid on your return. A compass is a necessity. In the sea caves, wear a helmet and exercise extreme caution.

LOGISTICS: The National Park Service plans to have a paddle-in campsite area on the east end of Santa Rosa Island by September 1990. Pack in your own water, and carry out your trash. Park your car in the neighborhood, not at the park. Bring two 50-foot lengths of rope, two 18-foot lengths of webbing tied in loops, and two caribiners to rig a heavy lift system at the Anacapa dock.

THE TRANSLUCENT SEA: Baja California and the Sea of Cortez, Mexico (pp. 193–202)

LOCATION: Mulegé, on the east coast of Baja California in the Mexican state of Baja California Sur, 615 miles south of Tijuana.

SEASON: October through May.

TRIP LENGTH: From 5 miles south of Mulegé, 75 miles to Loreto. Plan 10 days to 3 weeks or more. (Note: we stopped short of Loreto and were picked up by friends.)

DEGREE OF DIFFICULTY: Intermediate.

GETTING THERE/PUT-IN: By air to Loreto and bus north to Mulegé. By car from the San Diego area, take Highway 1 south to Mulegé. Put in on any beach where campers congregate, and inquire about a safe place to park your car. A suggested place is the Hotel Serenidad, 2 miles south of Mulegé.

INFORMATION/RESERVATIONS/ACCOMMODATIONS/GUIDES: For travel information, road conditions, and issues of safety for traveling into Baja, a must visit website is www.bajanet.com. Call your local Mexican consulate. Trudy Angel has been guiding this route for 24 years. Contact her at Paddling South, P.O. Box 827, Calistoga, California 94515, tel. (800) 398-6200, (707) 942-4550, www.paddlingsouth.com. (summertime), (707) 942-4550. The National Outdoor Leadership School (NOLS) has provided 2 weeks to 78 days (college credit) courses in Baja in kayaks, sailboats, and on land since 1971. Dates from October through April. NOLS: 288 Main Street, Lander, Wyoming 82520-3140, tel. (307) 332-6973, www.NOLS.EDU.

CAUTIONS: By car, take a full 10-gallon gas can across the border and buy gas whenever you can below San Quintin. Use extra-grade gas, because lower octane gas can damage your car's catalytic converter. Gas is least available between Santa Inez and Guerrero Negro. The highway has been improving steadily, but drive with extreme caution. Most important: do not drive at night because of cattle on the highway. Paddling: always strive for a predawn start to make distance. Carry as much water as possible.

LOGISTICS: Tourist permits are required and can be obtained at the nearest Mexican consulate or at the border (have your passport or a copy of your birth certificate with you). Gas up, change money, and buy Mexican car insurance—for the days you will be driving only—from drive-in booths in San Ysidro, California or other main border crossings. Water is available at Mulegé; plan for three quarts per day per person. Charts and maps of Baja have vastly improved since our first trips. Contact the California Map and Travel Center, 3312 Pico Blvd., Santa Monica, California 90405, tel. (310)396-6277, after checking out their list of maps on their website, www.travel.mapper.com, for what best suits your trip.

MANGROVE MAÑANA: La Manzanilla, Mexico (pp. 143-53)

LOCATION: The state of Jalisco on the Mexican west coast, 100 miles south of Puerto Vallarta.

SEASON: November to January.

TRIP LENGTH: Base camp paddling, 5 to 7 days.

DEGREE OF DIFFICULTY: Beginner.

GETTING THERE/PUT-IN: Fly to either Puerto Vallarta or Manzanillo and take the bus to La Manzanilla.

INFORMATION/RESERVATIONS/ACCOMMODATIONS: Contact the nearest Mexican consulate. Beach camping or *palapa* rental.

GUIDES: (Scott Roberge pulled out of La Manzanilla with the arrival of tourism proper, changing his company name to Tongass Kayak Adventures based out of Petersburg, Alaska, and now runs trips on the Stikine River, to the La Conte Glacier and Tebenkof Bay, P.O. Box 2169, Petersburg, Alaska 99833, tel. (907) 772-4600, www.tongasskayak.com).

CAUTIONS: Sunshine. La Manzanillo is now discovered, but it is still heaven. The road is paved; there's a golf course and at this writing a new hotel. The beach is still beautiful but this is a different trip. The mangroves are still good. If you camp on the beach, bury your valuables in the sand and remember where you buried them! Take care kayaking the passes between The Churches.

LOGISTICS: If you are on your own, depend upon the bus system. If you intend to stay over at a resort, try Melaque 20 miles south, or Manzanillo 30 miles south of that.

· GLOSSARY ·

Aleuts — the people of the Aleutian Islands in Alaska who, grouped with the Koniaq of Kodiak Island and the Chugach of mainland Alaska, depended on the kayak for their livelihood.

arroyo — the channel of a dry stream; a deep, dry gully.

baidarka — the word used by Russian explorers and fur traders for the Aleut kayak.

Beaufort scale — a method of equating wind velocity and wave conditions at sea to a numbered scale from 0–12 and a word description. For example, force three (7 to 10 knots) is described as a gentle breeze that will create large wavelets and scattered whitecaps. Force five (17 to 21 knots) is termed a fresh breeze with moderate waves taking a more pronounced, long form, with many whitecaps, and some spray.

bivouac — a temporary encampment, usually without shelter.

breakdown kayak — a kayak whose frame and fabric skin most closely resemble the original Aleut and Eskimo skin boats. Often called a portable or folding kayak, these boats are best for remote journeys necessitating backpacking or air travel.

broach — when a boat is turned sideways to the direction of the wave. In sea kayaking, usually caused by being caught in breaking surf.

cabrilla — a rockfish of the bass family common to Mexican waters.

ceviche — a traditional Mexican appetizer of raw fish marinated in lime juice, garlic, and salsa.

chine — the break between the side and bottom of a kayak's hull. Kayak designers speak of a "hard" or angular chine offering crisp handling, and a "soft" or rounded chine giving uniform stability.

close-hauled — a sailing term for when a vessel is sailing as close to the wind as she will go.

coaming — a raised frame around holes in the deck of a boat (as around a hatchway) to keep out water.

Escape — a high-volume, hard-chine kayak designed in 1980 by Mariner Kayaks in Kirkland, Washington.

Eskimo roll — a kayaking technique of righting oneself when capsized, by a sweep of the paddle and a snap of the kayaker's hips.

Feathercraft — a folding or breakdown kayak designed in Vancouver, British Columbia, made with aircraft aluminum, hypalon rubber, and Cordura fabric.

feathered — when a kayak paddle is fixed or adjusted in such a way that its two blades are opposed, that is, set at a ninety-degree angle to each other. This allows the paddle blade to "knife" the wind on a forward stroke and minimize resistance.

ferry glide — also called ferrying, a method of kayak navigation for crossing currents by paddling on an upstream angle to counter the force of the current while your forward progress actually takes you laterally to your destination.

Folbot — a beamy, high-volume breakdown kayak of laminated wood and rubberized canvas made by Folbot of Charleston, South Carolina.

force three, force five — see Beaufort scale.

four-cycle — the engine used in jet skis, a highly polluting engine.

Gel-coat — a common sea kayak construction process that produces a finished outer coating of pigmented

· GLOSSARY ·

fiberglass resin that is bonded to the hull and can chip with hard contact.

hard-shell kayak — any rigid, nonbreakdown kayak.

hole-in-the-wall arch — an arch created by waves refracting around both sides of a headland.

hypothermia — the loss of mental control and body function due to prolonged exposure to cold temperatures.

kayak — (as used in *The Hidden Coast*) a sea kayak that is large, long, and built for long-distance open-water travel, as opposed to the low-volume, highly maneuverable river or white-water kayaks.

Kelty — a well-known backpack especially popular in the 1970s.

lee — the opposite side from that against which the wind blows; the side sheltered from the wind.

Nautiraid — a French folding or breakdown sea kayak designed before World War II and made of laminated wood framing and a rubber-coated fabric skin.

pogies — mitten-shaped gloves for kayakers; they have an open palm to provide a sure grip which is Velcroed to close over the shaft of the paddle.

Polaris — (Polaris II) a medium-volume sea kayak designed by Dan Ruuska, who is known for his excellent workmanship and outspoken support of sea kayaking.

portage — the act of carrying boats and gear overland from one body of water to another.

reach — a straight portion of a stream or river.

serac — a large block or tower of ice created as a glacier flows and fractures down an incline or overrides an obstruction.

spray skirt — a skirtlike garment made of waterproof coated nylon and/or neoprene, which fits around both the kayaker's chest and the coaming of the kayak, making the cockpit watertight.

surfing — when sea kayakers utilize the slope and forward motion of a breaking wave to ride their kayaks at an accelerated rate of speed.

survival suits — full-body dry suits required for overwater flight on most helicopter sorties during the *Exxon Valdez* oil spill.

Thermarest cushion — a self-inflating seat pad or sleeping pad made by Cascade Designs of Seattle, Washington.

wave train — "train" or group of waves created by ocean swells as they travel from their source. Though an imperfect science, when surf landing, kayakers will watch the wave train for a pattern and then follow the biggest waves in.

Wind Dancer — The name of a sea kayak made by Eddyline Kayak Works that is known for its stability.

Zodiac — an inflatable breakdown or folding boat, powered by an outboard motor, that is especially useful at fly-in destinations.

Angell, Tony, and Kenneth C. Balcomb, III. *Marine Birds and Mammals of Puget Sound*. Washington Sea Grant Publication. Seattle: University of Washington Press, 1982.

Arima, E. Y. *The West Coast (Nootka) People*. Victoria, B.C.: British Columbia Provincial Museum, Special Publication #6, 1983.

Baeger, Johann Jakob, S.J. *Observations in Lower California*. Translated by M. M. Brandenburg and Carl L. Baumann. Berkeley: University of California Press, 1952.

Bascom, Willard. *Waves and Beaches*. Garden City, New Jersey: Doubleday, 1964.

Bent, Arthur Cleveland. *Life Histories of North American Birds, Marsh Birds*. New York: Dover Publications, 1963.

Botkin, Daniel B. *Our Natural History, the Lessons of Lewis and Clark*. New York: Berkeley Publishing Group, 1995.

Brenden, A., et al. "Columbia River Dams and the Decline of Northwest Salmon," University of Oregon, http//biology.uoregon.edu, 1998, 1–3.

Brookman, Al, Sr. *Sitka Man*. Anchorage: Alaska Northwest Publishing, 1984.

Carefoot, Thomas. *Pacific Seashores, A Guide to Intertidal Ecology*. Seattle: University of Washington Press, 1977.

Caughman, Madge, and Joanne S. Ginsberg. *California Coastal Resource Guide*. Berkeley: University of California Press, 1987.

Chapman, Charles F. *Piloting, Seamanship and Small Boat Handling*, Vol. 5. New York: Motor Boating, 1963–64 edition.

Coyle, Jeanette, and Norman C. Roberts. *A Field Guide to the Common and Interesting Plants of Baja California*. La Jolla, California: Natural History Publishing, 1975.

Dabberdt, Walter F. *Weather for Outdoorsmen*. New York: Charles Scribner's Sons, 1981.

Dalzell, Kathleen E. *The Queen Charlotte Islands*. Vol. 2: *Places and Names*. Queen Charlotte City, B.C.: Bill Ellis Publisher, 1981.

Davidson, Art. *In the Wake of the* Exxon Valdez. San Francisco: Sierra Club Books, 1989.

Department of the Interior. "Hanford Reach of the Columbia River, Draft River Conservation Study and Environmental Impact Statement." Washington, D.C., 1992.

Department of the Interior. "Hanford Reach of the Columbia River, Comprehensive River Conservation Study and Environmental Impact Statement," Vol. 1. Washington, D.C., 1994.

Dietrich, William. *Northwest Passage: The Great Columbia River*. Seattle: University of Washington Press, 1996.

Dowty, Karen Jones. *A Visitor's Guide: The California Channel Islands*. Ventura, California: Seaquit, 1984.

Duffus, David A. "Non-Consumptive Use and Management of Cetaceans in British Columbia Coastal Waters." Unpublished dissertation. University of Victoria, British Columbia, 1988.

Dyson, George. *Baidarka*. Edmonds, Washington: Alaska Northwest Publishing, 1986.

———. "An Illicit Alliance—The California Sea Kayaking Boom of 1803–1841." *Sea Kayaker* 4:1(Summer 1987):8–14.

Harden, Blaine. *A River Lost: The Life and Death of the Columbia River*. New York: W. W. Norton, 1996.

Hayden, Mike. *Exploring the North Coast*. San Francisco: Chronicle Books, 1982.

· BIBLIOGRAPHY ·

Howorth, Peter C. *Channel Islands, The Story Behind the Scenery.* Las Vegas: KC Publications, 1982.

Hoyt, Eric. *ORCA: A Whale Called Killer.* Ontario: Camden East, 1984.

Ince, John, and Hedi Kottner. *Sea Kayaking Canada's West Coast.* Vancouver: Raxas Books Inc., 1982.

Johnson, William Webber. *Baja California.* New York: Time-Life Books, 1972.

Kenyon, Karl W. *The Sea Otter in the Eastern Pacific Ocean.* New York: Dover Publications, 1975, p. 185.

Kirkendall, Tom, and Vicky Spring. *Bicycling the Pacific Coast.* Seattle: The Mountaineers, 1984.

Krause, Aurel. *The Tlingit Indians.* Translated by Erna Gunther. Seattle: University of Washington Press, 1956.

Lethcoe, Nancy R. *Glaciers of Prince William Sound, Alaska.* Valdez, Alaska: Prince William Sound Books, 1987.

Lewis, Meriwether, and William Clark. *The History of the Expedition under the Command of Lewis and Clark.* Edited by Elliot Coues. 4 vols. 1893. Reprint. New York: Dover Publications, 1998.

Lilly, Cdr. Kenneth E., Jr. NOAA. *Marine Weather of Western Washington.* Seattle: Starpath School of Navigation, 1983.

MacDonald, George F. *Haida Monumental Art: The Villages of the Queen Charlotte Islands.* Vancouver: University of British Columbia Press, 1983.
———. *Ninstints.* Museum Note #12. Vancouver: University of British Columbia Press, in association with the UBC Museum of Anthropology, 1983.

McCall, Lynne. *California's Chumash Indians.* Edited by Rosalind Perry, Santa Barbara, California: Santa Barbara Museum of Natural History, 1986.

McIntyre, Joan, ed. *Mind in the Waters.* New York: Charles Scribner's Sons; 1974.

Michaels, Leonard, David Reid, and Raquel Scherr, eds. *West of the West, Imagining California.* San Francisco: North Point Press, 1989.

Mickleson, Pete. *Natural History of Alaska's Prince William Sound and How To Enjoy It.* Cordova, Alaska: Alaska Wild Wings, 1989.

Miller, Pam. "Mangroves, On the Fringes of the Tropics." *Sea Kayaker* 6:3(Winter 1989–90):28–33.

Moziño, José Mariano. *Noticias de Nutka.* Translated and edited by Iris Higbie Wilson. Seattle: University of Washington Press, 1970.

National Ocean Service. *The United States Coast Pilot.* Vol. 7, *Pacific Coast: California, Oregon, Washington, and Hawaii.* 25th ed. Washington, D.C., 1989.

Northern California Atlas and Gazetteer. Freeport, Maine: DeLorme Mapping Co., 1988.

"Northwest Salmon at the Crossroads." *The High Country News* 23:27(1991): 6–28.

Ogden, Adele. *The California Sea Otter Trade 1784–1848.* Vol. 260 Berkeley: University of California Publications, 1941.

Pacific County and Its Resources. South Bend: Pacific County Board of Commissioners, 1909.

Paz, Octavio. *Selected Poems of Octavio Paz.* A bilingual edition with translations by Murie Rukeyser. Bloomington: Indiana University Press, 1968.

Peck, Cyrus E., Sr. *The Tides People, The Tlingit Indians of Southeast Alaska.* Juneau, Alaska: Juneau School District Indian Studies Program, 1975.

Peterson, Emil R., and Alfred Powers.

A Century of Coos and Curry. Portland, Oregon: Binfords and Mort, 1952.

Peterson, Lester R. "British Columbia's Depopulated Coast." In Howard White, ed., Raincoast Chronicles First Five. Madeira Park, B.C.: Harbour Publishing, 1976, 156–63.

Pethick, Derek. The Nootka Connection, Europe and the Northwest Coast 1790–1795. Vancouver: Douglas & McIntyre, 1980.

Pilot Chart of the North Pacific Ocean. PILOT558807. Washington, D.C.: The Defense Mapping Agency, July–September 1988.

Pilot Chart of the North Pacific Ocean. PILOT558904. Washington, D.C.: The Defense Mapping Agency, April–June, 1989.

Pyle, Robert Michael. Wintergreen. Boston: Houghton Mifflin, 1986.

Robbins, Chandler S., Bertel Bruun, and Herbert S. Zim. Birds of North America. New York: Golden Press, 1966.

Spong, Paul. "The Whale Show." In Joan McIntyre, ed. Mind in the Waters. New York: Charles Scribner's Sons, 1974.

Steinbeck, John. Log from the Sea of Cortez. New York: Penguin Books, 1986.

Swanton, John R. Contributions to the Ethnology of the Haida, The Jesup North Pacific Expedition, Vol. 5. 1905. Reprint. New York: The American Museum of Natural History, 1975.

The Nature Conservancy of Washington. Hanford Reach of the Columbia River, Proposed Wild and Scenic River Designation and National Wild Life Refuge. Seattle, 1998, 1–21.

The Nature Conservancy of Washington. Biodiversity Inventory and Analysis of the Hanford Site, Annual Report. Edited by Robert J. Pabst. Seattle, 1994.

Thompson, Richard E. Oceanography of the British Columbia Coast. Ottawa, Ontario: Department of Fisheries and Oceans, 1981.

U.S. Fish and Wildlife Service. "Total Marine Birds Retrieved Following the Exxon Valdez Oil Spill." Anchorage, December 19, 1989.

Van Arsdell, John. "B.C. Whaling: The Indians." In Howard White, ed., Raincoast Chronicles First Five. Madeira Park, B.C.: Harbour Publishing, 1976.

Warshall, Peter. "The Ways of Whales." In Joan McIntyre, ed., Mind in the Waters. New York: Charles Scribner's Sons, 1974.

Washburne, Randel. Kayak Trips in Puget Sound and the San Juan Islands. Seattle: Pacific Search Press, 1986.

Washington Atlas and Gazetteer. Freeport, Maine: DeLorme Mapping Co., 1988.

Washington State Department of Natural Resources. "Our Changing Nature: Natural Resource Trends in Washington State." Olympia, Washington. 1998.

Wood, Charles E. Charlie's Charts of the Western Coast of Mexico Including Baja. Surrey, B.C.: Charlie's Charts, 1968.

Woodbridge, Sally B., and John M. Woodbridge. Architecture, San Francisco, The Guide. San Francisco: 101 Productions, 1982.

Zorpette, Glenn. "Confronting the Nuclear Legacy, Part II." Scientific American 274:5(May 1996): 88–97.

· INDEX ·

Bold page numbers indicate maps; *italic* page numbers indicate illustrations; (n) indicates chapter notes.

Alaska: bush planes in, 29–33, 84; machines in, 29. *See also* Chichagof Island; Prince William Sound
Alava, Cape, 103, 108
Aleut people, 11, 188–89
Anacapa Island, 181–91, **182,** 217–18(n); access to, 229; caves of, *154,* 190–91
Aquatic Park, 125
Astoria Bridge, 163
Astoria, Oregon, 163–64

Baja California, *155,* 193–202, **194,** 218(n); access to, 230; geological history of, 195; packing for kayaking in, 197; plant life in, 199; rainfall in, 199, 200; wildlife in, 200
Bajo Point, 69
Barkley Sound, 76
Barry Arm, 25–26, *81*
Barry Glacier, 26
Bartlett Island, 76
Bay of Isles, 19, *82*
Bays, 113
Bears, 39–40, 53
Bella Bella people, 43
Bella Coola people, 43
Blackfish Sound, 55–66, 88–89, 214–15(n)
Blackney Pass, 62
Bligh Island, 70, *92*
Blunden Island, 76
Bonneville Dam, 134
Boom Slough, 96, 101
Boston Point, 69, 70
breakdown kayaks, 33–34
British Columbia. *See* Johnstone Strait; Nootka Sound; Queen Charlotte Islands

Broken Islands, 76
Brooks Peninsula, 76
Bunsby Islands, 76
Burdwood Point, 75
Burnaby Island, 50
bush planes, 29–33, *84*
Bybee Ledge Channel, 161

cacti, *155, 200*
California. *See* Anacapa Island; Lost Coast; San Francisco Bay; Santa Barbara Channel Islands
California, Gulf of. *See* Cortez, Sea of
canoes, early, 43
Cape Disappointment light, 165, 167
Cape Horn, 161
Cascade Glacier, 26
Cathedral Cave, 190, 191
Cathlamet, Washington, 161, 162
Caution Pass, 41
Caves: Anacapa Island, *154,* 190–91; Sea Lion Caves, 175, 177
Channel Islands National Park, 183, 186
Charleston, Oregon, 122
Chichagof Island, 29–41, **30,** *85,* 214(n); access to, 220; White Sulphur Hot Springs, 40, *84*
chip ships, 118, *149*
Chugach Range, 20, 22
Chumash people, 11
Churches, the, *158,* 207
Clatsop Spit, 164, 167
Clayoquot Sound, 76, *94*
clearcutting: Coos River, 119, 121; Queen Charlotte Islands fight against, 46–47; Robson Bight fight against, 60
Coast Pilot, 173, 217(n)
Coast Salish people, 43
College Fjord, 21, 22

Columbia River, **128,** *150, 151,* 216–17(n); access to, 226, 227; birds of, 131–32; dams, 127, 129, 134; fish spawning grounds, 132–34; Hanford Reach, 127–38, 168; lower Columbia, 143–44, 161–68; mouth of, 164–68; Portland, 138–41; wildlife of, 131, 132
Concepción, Bahía de, *156,* 197
Cook Channel, 70, 76
Coos Bay, Oregon, **114,** 118–22; access to, 225; timber industry in, 118–22
Coos River, 119–22, *149;* clearcutting in valley, 119, 121; forks of, 120
Copper Bay, *82, 83*
Cortez, Sea of, *155,* 193–202, **194,** 218(n); access to, 230; geological history of area, 195; sea life in, 198
Coxe Glacier, 26
Culross Passage, 20
Cumshewa Inlet, 54

De Havilland Otter, 31–33, 84
Devil's Elbow State Park, 175–77
Diablo, Point, 124
Dodge Point, 50
Dolomite Narrows, 47, 49, *87*
Doolth Mountain, 35, *84*
Doran, Point, 25–26, 27
Dry Pass, 40, 41, *85*
Dunlin, 94–95, 101

Eel River, 172
egrets, 211
El Coyoté Bay, *156*
elk, 118
Eshamy Bay, 20
Esperanza Inlet, 76
Estevan, Point, 69
Exxon Valdez, 17–21, 27, *82*

· INDEX ·

Fairweather Range, 38
farmlands along Columbia River, 134
Feathercraft kayaks, 33–34
floatplanes, 29–33, 84
Florence, Oregon, 175
fog, kayaking in, 173
food, road, 169, 177–78
Fort Canby State Park, 167
Fraser River, 55
Freshwater Slough, 79
Friendly Cove, 70–71, 72, 73, 75
fucus seaweed, 35, 85

garter snakes, 95
glaciers, 26
Gold River, 67, 76
Golden Gate Bridge, 122–24, 148
Goode, Mount, 22
Graham Island, 46
Grand Coulee dam, 134
Granite Islands, 37
Gray's Bay, 164
grebes, 24
guides, sea kayaking, 36. See also tours, kayaking
Gulf of California. See Cortez, Sea of
gunkholing, 169

Haida people, 43, 46, 47–49, 86, 87. See also longhouses
Hanford Reach, 127–38, 168, 216(n), 226
Hanford Site, 130, 134–35
Hanson Island, 58, 61
harlequins, 24
Harriman Fjord, 21, 22, 23, 25–26
Harrington Point Range, 164
Hawkins Island, 20
Hecata Head, 170, 175–77, 228
Hecate Strait, 50
herons, 159, 209, 210
Highway 101, 175

Hinchinbrook Island, 20
Hobo Bay, 23, 24, 28
Hot Springs Cove, 76

Inside Passage, 57

jellyfish, 84
Jim Crow Point, 163
Johnstone Strait, 55–66, 56, 214–15(n); access to, 221; boundaries of, 55; bull kelp, 90; orcas in, 55–58; salmon in, 55–57
Junkyard Beach, 201

Kalama Upper Range, 161
Kalama, Washington, 144
Kayak Express, 19, 21, 22
kayaking: demographics of kayakers, 13; growth and history of, 11–13, 212; in big waves, 38–39, 73–74, 109–11; in fog, 173; in following seas, 51; in wind, 36–37, 51, 122–23, 161–62; rescues, 8–10. See also tours, kayaking
kayaks: breakdown, 33–34; forerunners of, 43; history of, 11–13. See also kayaking
kelp, bull, 90
Kennewick, Washington, 135
Knight Island, 17–19, 82, 83
Knight Island Passage, 20
Koniaq people, 20–21
Kwakiutl people, 43, 62
Kyoquot Sound, 76

La Manzanilla, Jalisco, 158, 203–11, 204, 231
La Push, Washington, 103, 147
Lake Umatilla, 138
Latouche Island, 20
Lime Point, 123–24
longhouses, 45, 48, 50, 52, 86
Lost Coast, 152–53, 169–74, 170, 217(n), 228

Lost Island, 47, 50, 51
Lower Columbia River, 143–44, 161–68
Lyell Island, 50

machines in Alaska, 29
Makah Bay, 105
Makah people, 105, 108
mangrove swamps, 159, 208–11
Maquinna Point, 74
Marcus Baker, Mount, 22
Marshfield Channel, 121
Masset, British Columbia, 46
Mattole people, 174
Mattole River, 152–53, 172, 173
McNary Dam, 138
McNary Pool, 136–38
Meares, Cape, 152, 170, 177–80, 229
Mexico, Pacific coast of, 160. See also Baja California; La Manzanilla, Jalisco
middens, 45
Millicoma River, 120
Milltown, Washington, 79, 97
Moachaht people, 71, 73
Montague Island, 20
Moresby Camp, 54
Moresby Island, 46–47, 49–50
Muchalat Inlet, 67–69
muddy banks, 117
Mulegé, Mexico, 196
Multnomah Channel, 142
Myriad Islands, 39

Naked Island, 19
Narrow Strait village, 50
Nautiraid kayaks, 33
Neah Bay, 105
Netarts Bay, 178
Nez Perce people, 136
Ninstints, British Columbia, 47–49, 86
Nootka Convention of 1792, 72
Nootka Island, 70

238

· INDEX ·

Nootka Sound, 67–76, **68,** 92, 93, 215(n); access to, 222; history of, 70–71, 72–73; native people of, 71; on early maps, 70
North Bend, Oregon, 119, 122, 149
North Inian Pass, 32
North Jetty of the Columbia, 164, 166, 167
Northern California coast, 152–53, 169–74, **170,** 217(n)
Northern Lights Expeditions, 60
nuclear reactors, 130

Oceanside, Oregon, 153, 178
Ogden Passage, 39
oil rig "Gina," 184
oil spills, Exxon Valdez, 17–21, 82
old-growth forests, on Queen Charlotte Islands, 46–47
Olympic National Park, 105
Olympic Peninsula coast, 103–11, **104,** 145–46, 147, 215(n); access to, 223–24; geology of, 103; native people of, 71
orcas, 24, 25, 61–66, 88–89; activities of, 63–66; hunting of, 214(n); in Johnstone Strait, 55–58; study of, 57–59, 214–15(n)
Oregon coast, 217(n). See also Coos Bay, Oregon; Hecata Head; Meares, Cape
Oregon Dunes, 122
otters, sea, 26–27, 214(n); communities of, 188–89; hunting of, 189, 217–18(n); natural history of, 216–17(n)
Outback Expeditions, 206
Ozette archaeological site, 108

Pacific Coast, **12**

Pacific County Museum, 113, 115
Pacific Rim National Park, 76
Pasco, Washington, 135
pelapas, 203, 208
pelicans, 201
Petrolia, California, 172
Pigot Point, 22
pinnacle waves, 73
plutonium, 132
Point of Arches, 105, 106–9
Port Wells, 21, 22–28, 23, 82
Portage Head, 106
Portland, Oregon, 138–41, 227
Portlock Harbor, 39
Presidio, the, 125
Priest Rapids Dam, 129
Prince of Tokyo II (chip ship), 118, 149
Prince William Sound, 17–28, **18,** 81, 82, 83; access to, 219; effects of oil spill on, 17–21, 20, 27, 82; rain in, 22, 23
Puget Island Reach and Turn, 163
Punta Concepción, 197
Punta Gorda, 173–74

QG 7 bell, 166, 217(n)
Queen Charlotte City, British Columbia, 46, 47
Queen Charlotte Islands, 43–54, **44,** 86, 87, 214(n); access to, 220; archaeological sites of, 45; fight against clearcutting, 46–47; old-growth forests of, 46–47; sea life of, 49–50, 87; wildlife of, 45–46

Rattlesnake Ridge, 132
ravens, 38
Richland, Washington, 135
road food, 169, 177–78
Robson Bight, 59–60, 90, 221
Rogue waves, 110, 215(n)

rooster fish, 156
Rose Harbour, 47
Russian explorers, 32
Russian-American Company, 188

salmon: Hanford Reach habitat protection, 132–34, 168, 216(n); in Johnstone Strait, 55–57
salt grasses, 100, 101
San Basilio Bay, 202
San Francisco Bay, **114,** 122–25, 148, 225
San Francisco, California, 124–25
San Juanico Cove, 157, 201–2
San Miguel Island, 183, 186
San Nicolas Island, 189
Sand Island, 164–65
sand prairies, 80
Sandspit, British Columbia, 46
Santa Barbara Channel Islands, 181–91, **182,** 217–18(n); access to, 229; history of, 186, 188–89
Santa Barbara Island, 186
Santa Cruz Island, 183
Santa Rosa Island, 183, 186
Sauvie Island, 142
Sea Kayaker magazine, 13
sea kayaking. See kayaking; kayaks
Sea Kayaking (John Dowd), 13
Sea Level Slough, 41
Sea Lion Caves, 175, 177
sea lions, 153, 175, 177, 179
Sea of Cortez. See Cortez, Sea of
sea stars, 85
seaweed: bull kelp, 90; fucus, 35, 85
shanties, sea, 105, 107, 108, 111, 215(n)
Shi Shi Beach, 103–11, 215(n), 223–24
Sierra de la Giganta, 156

· INDEX ·

silverweed, 118
Skagit River, 77–79, 97–101
Skagit River estuary, 77–79, **78,** 97–101, 215(n); access to, 222–23; bird life of, 94–95, 96, 99, 100, 101; plant life of, 98, 99, 100, 101; tides in, 80, 97; wildlife of, 77, 95, 96, 98, 99
Skamokawa Channel Range, 163
Skana (first captive orca), 58, 214(n)
Skedans, British Columbia, 47, 52–54, 87
Skidegate, British Columbia, 46
Smith Island, 19
Snake River, 135
snakes, garter, 95
snow geese, 100, 215(n)
Sooes River, 105
South Bend, Washington, 115
South Moresby Island, 50
South Moresby National Park Reserve, 46
South Slough National Estuarine Reserve, 122
Southwinds Sports Resource kayak tours, 183
Spencer, Cape, 32
Spirit Walker Expeditions, 34
St. Helens, Oregon, 142–43
Starship and the Canoe, The (Kenneth Brower), 14
Steamboat Reach, 163
Steamboat Slough, 79, 96, 97
steller's sea lions, 52, 175, 177

Tahsis Inlet, 76
Tahsis Inlet villages, 71
Tanu village, 50
Telegraph Cove, 59–60, *91,* 221
Tenacatita, Bahía, 207
Three Arch Rocks, *153,* 178–80
tides in Skagit River Estuary, 80, 97
Tillamook Bay, 178
timber industry: Coos Bay, 118–22; Queen Charlotte Islands, 46–47, 54; Robson Bight, 60; South Bend, Washington, 115
Tlingit people, 32, 38, 43, 214(n)
Tom Moore Slough, 79, 97
tomols, 11
totem poles, 47–48, 52–53, 86, 93
tours, kayaking, 36; Northern Lights Expeditions, 60; Outback Expeditions, 206; Southwinds Sports Resource, 183; Spirit Walker Expeditions, 34
Tri-Cities area, 135
Tsimshian people, 43

Uchuck III, 67–69, 93
Umatilla, Oregon, 138

Valhalla, Mount, 22
Vancouver Island, 55, 94; native people of, 71; Pacific coast of, 76. *See also* Nootka Sound; Robson Bight

Vernita Bridge, 129
Vizcaino Desert, 196
Vorota Island, 36

Wahluke Slope, 134–35
Wallula Gap, 136–37
Washington. *See* Olympic Peninsula coast; Skagit River estuary; Willapa Bay
Washington Kayak Club, 11
waves: kayaking in, 38–39, 73–74, 109–11; pinnacle waves, 73; rogue waves, 110, 215(n)
Welch Island Reach, 163
Wells Passage, 21
Westcoast people, 43, 69, 71, 72–73
Weynton Passage, 61, 64, 65
whales. *See* orcas
White Bluffs, 130, 131–32, 134
White Sulphur Hot Springs, 40, 84
Whittier, Alaska, 22
Willamette River, 139–42, 227
Willapa Bay, 113–18, **114;** access to, 224; plant and wildlife, 118; tributary rivers of, 116, *148*
wind, kayaking in, 36–37, 51, 122–23, 161–62

Yakima people, 136
Yakima River, 135
Yakobi Island, 32
yellowlegs, greater, 94–95
Yuquot, British Columbia, 70, 71–73, 75, 93, 215(n)